# Contents

i

# Contents

Name _____

# Strategy Workshop

As you listen to the story "The Rule," by Anne Cameron, you will stop from time to time to do some activities on these practice pages. These activities will help you think about different strategies that can help you read better. After completing each activity, you will discuss what you've written with your classmates and talk about how to use these strategies.

Remember, strategies can help you become a better reader. Good readers

- use strategies whenever they read

- use different strategies before, during, and after reading

- think about how strategies will help them

Name _____

## Strategy 1: Predict/Infer

Use this strategy before and during reading to help make predictions about what happens next or what you're going to learn.

Here's how to use the Predict/Infer strategy:

1. Think about the title, the illustrations, and what you have read so far.
2. Tell what you think will happen next—or what you will learn. Thinking about what you already know about the subject may help.
3. Try to figure out things the author does not say directly.

Listen as your teacher begins "The Rule." When your teacher stops, complete the activity with a partner to show that you understand how to predict what you think might happen in the story.

Think about the story and respond to the question below.

What do you think might happen in the story?

_____

_____

As you continue listening to the story, think about whether your prediction was right. You might want to change your prediction or write a new one below.

_____

_____

_____

Name _____

## Strategy 2: Phonics/Decoding

Use this strategy during reading when you come across a word you don't know.

Here's how to use the Phonics/Decoding strategy:

1. Look carefully at the word.
2. Look for word parts that you know and think about the sounds for the letters.
3. Blend the sounds to read the word.
4. Ask yourself if this is a word you know and whether the word makes sense in the sentence.
5. If not, ask yourself if there is anything else you could try—should you look in the dictionary?

Listen as your teacher continues to read the story. When your teacher stops, use the Phonics/Decoding strategy.

Now write down the steps you used to decode the word *trout*.

_____

_____

_____

_____

_____

_____

Remember to use this strategy whenever you are reading and come across a word that you don't know.

Name _____

## Strategy 3: Monitor/Clarify

Use this strategy during reading whenever you're confused about what you are reading.

Here's how to use the Monitor/Clarify strategy:
- Ask yourself if what you're reading makes sense—or if you are learning what you need to learn.
- If you don't understand something, reread, look at the illustrations, or read ahead to see if that helps.

Listen as your teacher continues to read the story. When your teacher stops, complete the activity with a partner to show that you understand how to figure out why the boy in the story might think the mushrooms look like a forest.

Think about the story and respond below.

1. Have you ever eaten mushrooms? What do they look like?

_____

_____

2. Can you tell from listening to the story why the boy may have thought the mushrooms looked like a forest? Why or why not?

_____

_____

3. How can you find out why he may have thought that?

_____

_____

Name _____

## Strategy 4: Question

Use this strategy during and after reading to ask questions about important ideas in the story.

Here's how to use the Question strategy:

- Ask yourself questions about important ideas in the story.
- Ask yourself if you can answer these questions.
- If you can't answer the questions, reread and look for answers in the text. Thinking about what you already know and what you've read in the story may help you.

Listen as your teacher continues to read the story. Then complete the activity with a partner to show that you understand how to ask yourself questions about important ideas in the story.

Think about the story and respond below.

Write a question you might ask yourself at this point in the story.

_____

_____

_____

_____

_____

If you can't answer your question now, think about it while you listen to the rest of the story.

Name _____

## Strategy 5: Evaluate

Use this strategy during and after reading to help you form an opinion about what you read.

Here's how to use the Evaluate strategy:

- Think about how the author makes the story come alive and makes you want to read it.
- Think about what was entertaining, informative, or useful about the selection.
- Think about how you reacted to the story—how well you understood the selection and whether you enjoyed reading it.

Listen as your teacher continues to read the story. When your teacher stops, complete the activity with a partner to show that you are thinking of how you feel about what you are reading and why you feel that way.

Think about the story and respond below.

1. Tell whether or not you think this story is entertaining and why.

_____

_____

2. This is a humorous, realistic fiction story. Did the author make the characters interesting and believable?

_____

_____

3. How did you react to this story?

_____

Name _____

## Strategy 6: Summarize

Use this strategy after reading to summarize what you read.

Here's how to use the Summarize strategy:
- Think about the characters.
- Think about where the story takes place.
- Think about the problem in the story and how the characters solve it.
- Think about what happens in the beginning, middle, and end of the story.

Think about the story you just listened to. Complete the activity with a partner to show that you understand how to identify important story parts that will help you summarize the story.

Think about the story and respond to the questions below:

1. Who is the main character?

_____

_____

2. Where does the story take place?

_____

_____

3. What is the problem and how is it resolved?

_____

_____

Now use this information to summarize the story for a partner.

Name _____

# Off to Adventure!

**Cut out a picture of something you think is an adventure from a magazine or a newspaper. Paste it on this page. Then answer the questions below.**

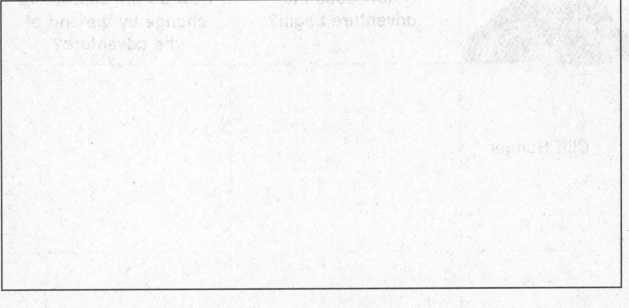

1. What do you think makes this an adventure?

_____

_____

2. How would you describe this adventure to someone?

_____

_____

3. Would you like to be part of this adventure? Explain your answer.

_____

_____

Name _____

# Off to Adventure!

**As you read each selection in *Off to Adventure!*, fill in the boxes of the chart that apply to the selection.**

|  | How does the adventure begin? | How do the characters change by the end of the adventure? |
|---|---|---|
| **Cliff Hanger** |  |  |
| **The Ballad of Mulan** |  |  |
| **The Lost and Found** |  |  |

Name _____

# Adventure Advertisement

**Help rewrite this ad to make it more exciting. Replace the words in parentheses with words from the box. Fill in the blanks with the correct words.**

Try rock climbing in the Teton Mountains! After you

have _____ (made a slow and difficult

journey on foot) to the base of a cliff, put on your

_____ (set of straps that can attach to a

safety rope). Make sure to climb on _____

(tied to a person or a rock with a rope for safety) so

you don't fall. If you get tired on the way up, find a

_____ (shelf of rock) and take a rest.

Then get ready for your _____ (a trip

down into or from something, such as a mountain). If

you really want a thrill, you can _____

(climb down from a steep height) back to the ground.

## Vocabulary

1. belay
2. descent
3. harness
4. ledge
5. rappel
6. trekked

**Describe how to rappel. (Hint: If you need help, look at pages 16–17 in your textbook.)**

_____

_____

Name _____

# Cause-and-Effect Chart

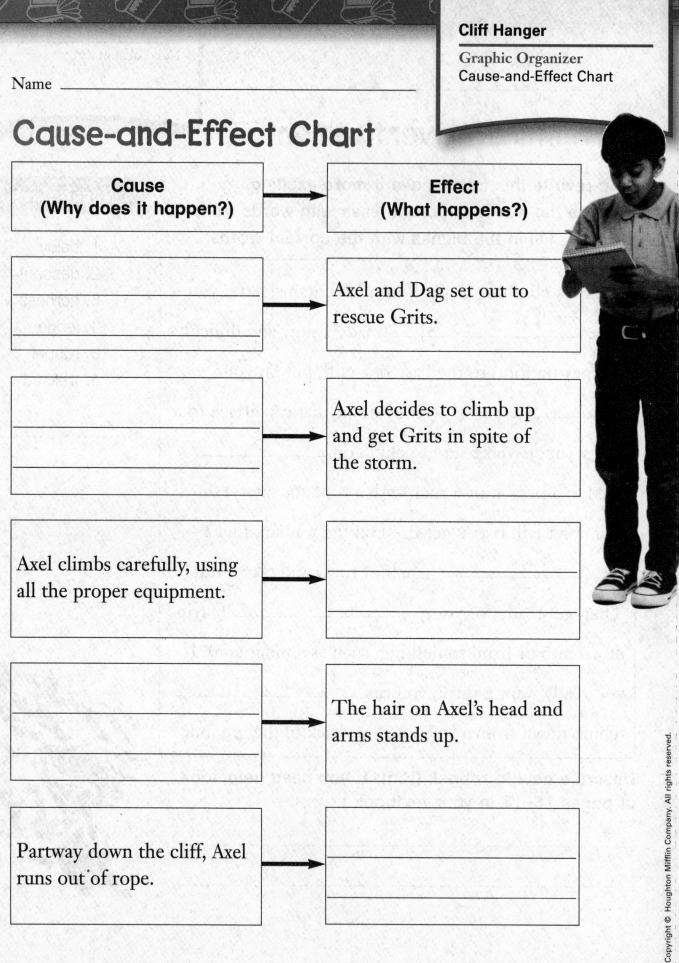

| Cause (Why does it happen?) | Effect (What happens?) |
|---|---|
| | Axel and Dag set out to rescue Grits. |
| | Axel decides to climb up and get Grits in spite of the storm. |
| Axel climbs carefully, using all the proper equipment. | |
| | The hair on Axel's head and arms stands up. |
| Partway down the cliff, Axel runs out of rope. | |

Name _____

# Finish the Story

**Complete each of the sentences with details from**
*Cliff Hanger.*

1. Axel's dog, Grits, _____

   _____

2. Dag tells Axel that the storm is still far enough away

   _____

   _____

3. Dag changes his mind and tells Axel not to climb, but

   _____

   _____

4. Axel reaches Grits safely and _____

   _____

5. He lowers Grits down on a rope, but _____

   _____

6. Axel rappels halfway down and _____

   _____

Name _____

# Causes and Effects

**Read the story. Think about what happens and why.
Then complete the chart on the next page.**

## The Tornado

A rooster crowed, waking Lucy Sunders from a deep sleep.
She usually popped out of bed like buttons pop off a shirt, but
today she was tired. She had stayed up late last night reading.

Lucy looked out her window. The sky was a funny yellow-
gray, and there were no sounds. Then, across the fields, Lucy
saw a whirling dust cloud. It grew bigger and bigger. A
tornado was coming!

Lucy raced down the stairs, shouting, "Mama, Mama —
a tornado!"

Mrs. Sunders checked the sky. Then she grabbed the baby
from his swing. "Run! Run to the root cellar!" she shouted.

Lucy and her mother ran through the yard, and Lucy
pulled open the cellar door. She hurried down the steps. Her
mother locked the door and followed her into the darkness.

Quickly Mrs. Sunders lit the old lamp, and the light
glowed warmly. Lucy sighed. They were safe now.
Everything would be all right.

Name _____

# Causes and Effects continued

**In each box, write a cause or an effect from the story.**

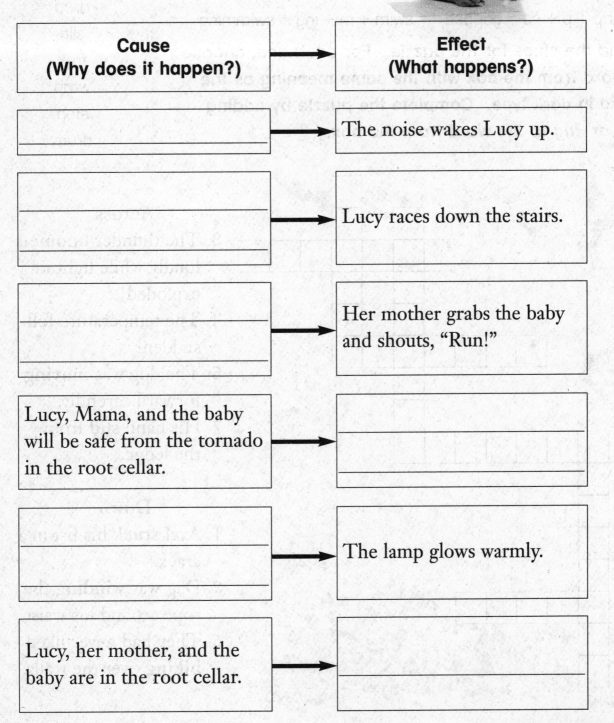

| Cause (Why does it happen?) | Effect (What happens?) |
|---|---|
| | The noise wakes Lucy up. |
| | Lucy races down the stairs. |
| | Her mother grabs the baby and shouts, "Run!" |
| Lucy, Mama, and the baby will be safe from the tornado in the root cellar. | |
| | The lamp glows warmly. |
| Lucy, her mother, and the baby are in the root cellar. | |

**Cliff Hanger**

Structural Analysis
Inflected Endings

# Add the Ending

▶ For words that end with a vowel and a single consonant, double the consonant before adding *-ed* or *-ing*.

grip + p + ed = gripped    swim + m + ing = swimming

**Read the clues for the puzzle. For each one, choose a word from the box with the same meaning as the word in dark type. Complete the puzzle by adding *-ed* or *-ing* to the word from the box.**

**Word Bank**

jam
drop
slip
trek
wrap
step
drum

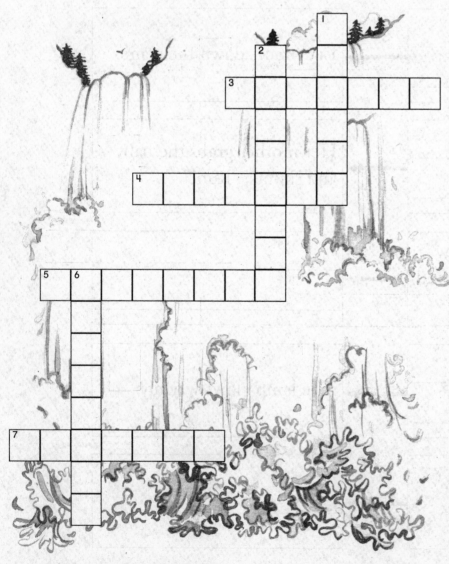

## Across

3. The thunder **boomed** loudly while lightning exploded.
4. The temperature **fell** suddenly.
5. The dog was **moving** forward carefully.
7. His hand **slid** from the ledge.

## Down

1. Axel **stuck** his fist in a crack.
2. Dag was **winding** the rope around his waist.
6. They had never liked **hiking** over the trails.

Name _____

# Short Vowels

▶ A short vowel sound is usually spelled with one
   vowel followed by a consonant sound.
   The /ă/ sound is usually spelled **a,** as in la**st.**
   The /ĕ/ sound is usually spelled **e,** as in sm**e**ll.
   The /ĭ/ sound is usually spelled **i,** as in m**i**x.

▶ Sometimes the /ĕ/ sound is spelled in a different way.
   In the starred words *head* and *friend*, the /ĕ/ sound is
   spelled *ea* and *ie*.

**Write each Spelling Word under its vowel sound.**

**Spelling Words**

1. mix*
2. milk
3. smell
4. last
5. head
6. friend*
7. class
8. left
9. thick
10. send
11. thin
12. stick

**/ă/ Sound**                    **/ĭ/ Sound**

_____          _____

_____          _____

**/ĕ/ Sound**                    _____

_____          _____

_____

_____

_____

_____

Name _____

# Spelling Spree

**Silly Rhymes**  Write a Spelling Word to complete each silly sentence.  Each answer rhymes with the underlined word.

1. Will chewing gum _____ to a <u>brick</u>?
2. Don't pile <u>bread</u> on your _____!
3. Never drink _____ while wearing <u>silk</u>.
4. You have to be _____ to squeeze under a <u>bin</u>.
5. <u>Fix</u> the ladder and _____ the batter.
6. How can you <u>tell</u> if bees can _____?

1. _____    4. _____

2. _____    5. _____

3. _____    6. _____

**Letter Math**  Write a Spelling Word by adding and taking away letters from the words below.

**Example:** d + fish - f = *dish*

7. spend - p        = _____

8. c + glass - g     = _____

9. leg - g + ft      = _____

10. fri + mend - m   = _____

11. blast - b        = _____

12. th + sick - s    = _____

Name _____

# Proofreading and Writing

**Proofreading** **Circle the five misspelled Spelling Words in the following notice. Then write each word correctly.**

1. mix*
2. milk
3. smell
4. last
5. head
6. friend*
7. class
8. left
9. thick
10. send
11. thin
12. stick

### Attention All Visitors

People come from many countries to hike in our wilderness areas and smel the clean mountain air. Please show your respect for this natural world. Be careful on the trails, and always hike with a freind. A hiking stik is a good idea too. Bring a thik sweater, and wear a hat to protect your hed from rain or sun. Enjoy your visit!

1. _____    4. _____

2. _____    5. _____

3. _____

**Write a Journal Entry** Think about a special time you had outdoors. Where were you? Was it a field trip? A family outing? Or maybe a block party?

**On a separate sheet of paper, describe where you were and what was special about the experience. Use Spelling Words from the list.**

Name _____

# Find the Right Order

**The words on List 1 appear in any old order.  Put the words in alphabetical order and write them on List 2.**

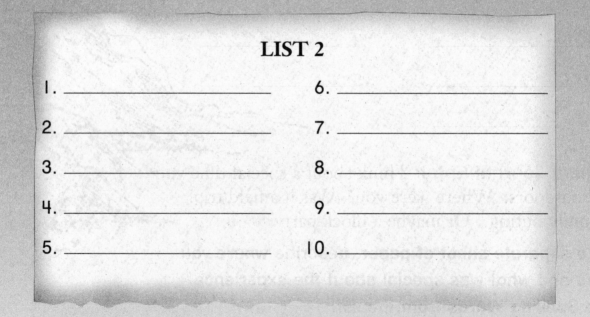

## LIST 1

| bottom | problem |
|--------|---------|
| pocket | stream |
| secure | cloud |
| mistake | boulder |
| ballet | ground |

## LIST 2

1. _____    6. _____

2. _____    7. _____

3. _____    8. _____

4. _____    9. _____

5. _____    10. _____

Name _____

# Finding Sentences

**Read each group of words. Write *sentence* if the words form a complete sentence. Write *fragment* if the words do not form a complete sentence. Then rewrite each fragment as a complete sentence. Add a word from the box at the bottom of the page.**

1. A big storm was coming fast. _____

_____

2. The frightened dog. _____

_____

3. Climbed slowly up the ledge. _____

_____

4. Axel saved Grits. _____

_____

5. A bolt of lightning. _____

_____

6. Heated on the stove. _____

_____

**Word Bank**

| Dag | Axel | Grits |
|-----|------|-------|
| soup | asked | flashed |
| rained | clouds | howled |

Name _____

# Changing Fragments into Sentences

**Correct each fragment below to make a complete sentence.**

1. Axel and his father

_____

2. was worried about his dog

_____

3. in the sky

_____

4. carried gear for rock climbing

_____

5. down the trail

_____

6. a dangerous ledge

_____

7. lots of rain

_____

8. had a big adventure that day

_____

# Finding Sentences

**Effective writers use complete sentences. Correct each
sentence fragment. Write your revised sentence on the line.
If the sentence is already complete, write the word** *correct*.

### A Day in the Life of Grits

1. I went for a walk. On a steep trail.

_____

2. In the warm sunshine, I wagged my tail.

_____

3. Then I heard thunder.

_____

4. The sky. Grew dark.

_____

5. Whimpered, howled, and barked.

_____

6. Then Axel climbed. Up the rock.

_____

I would thank him
if I could talk!

7. Hugged me.

_____

8. I felt safe.

_____

# Reasons and Facts

**Use this page to plan your explanation. Then number
your reasons or facts in the order you will use them.**

Topic: _____

_____

_____

Topic Sentence: _____

_____

_____

Reason/Fact: _____         Reason/Fact: _____

_____         _____

_____         _____

Reason/Fact: _____         Reason/Fact: _____

_____         _____

_____         _____

Name _____

# Improving Your Writing

► Sometimes questions can be changed into statements by moving the words around.

Are the children's parents good climbers?

The children's parents are good climbers.

► Sometimes words must be added, removed, or changed to make a question into a statement.

Did most readers like the story?

Most readers liked the story.

► Changing the question on a test into a statement can help you write a good topic sentence and focus your ideas.

Why is climbing exciting?

There are several reason why climbing is exciting.

**Change each question into a statement.**

1. What are some of the family's favorite activities?

_____

2. Did everyone in the class like the action story?

_____

3. Who are the main characters in this story?

_____

_____

4. Why is swimming under a waterfall fun?

_____

5. What types of movies does their family like to see?

_____

Name _____

# Revising Your Personal Narrative

**Reread your paper. Put a checkmark in the box for each sentence that describes your paper. Use this page to help you revise.**

### Rings the Bell

☐ The beginning catches the reader's interest.

☐ Many details and exact words bring the story to life.

☐ Everything is told in order and keeps to the topic.

☐ My writing sounds like me. You can tell how I feel.

☐ Sentences are different lengths. There are few mistakes.

### Getting Stronger

☐ The beginning could be more interesting.

☐ More details and exact words are needed.

☐ A few events are out of order, and a few are unrelated.

☐ My voice could be stronger. It doesn't always sound like me.

☐ Many sentences are short. There are some mistakes.

### Try Harder

☐ The beginning is missing or weak.

☐ There are no details or exact words.

☐ The story is not focused. The order is unclear.

☐ I can't hear my voice at all.

☐ All my sentences are short. Mistakes make it hard to read.

Name _____

# Combining Sentences

**Combine each pair of sentences into one. Include all the important parts of both sentences. Avoid repeating words.**

1. The water was cold. The water was full of sharks.

   _____

   _____

2. Nina dove in the water. Brenda dove in the water.

   _____

   _____

3. Paul screamed. Winston screamed.

   _____

4. Nina laughed. Nina shouted, "Come on in, fellas!"

   _____

   _____

5. Paul said, "No way!" Winston said, "No way!"

   _____

   _____

6. Brenda yelled, "These sharks are only toys!" Nina yelled, "These sharks are only toys!"

   _____

   _____

Name _____

# Spelling Words

Look for spelling patterns you have learned to help you remember the Spelling Words on this page. Think about the parts that you find hard to spell.

**Write the missing letters and apostrophe in the Spelling Words below.**

1. hav _____

2. hav _____ _____ _____ _____

3. f _____ _____ nd

4. ar _____ _____ nd

5. _____ ne

6. th _____ n

7. th _____ n

8. th _____ m

9. befo_____ _____

10. bec _____ _____ _____ e

11. _____ ther

12. _____ _____ ther

**Study List  On another sheet of paper, write each Spelling Word.  Check the list to be sure you spell each word correctly.**

Name _____

# Spelling Spree

**Sentence Fillers** Write the Spelling Word from the list on this page that best completes each sentence.

1–2. "Scott, _____ you seen my coat?"

"No, I _____."

3. We drove _____ the block three times.

4. Our neighbors asked us to lend _____ our lawnmower.

5. For a while it was noisy, but _____ it got quiet.

6. We met at the theater _____ the movie started.

7. I don't want this one, I want the _____ one.

8. Tania _____ a five-dollar bill lying on the ground.

1. _____    5. _____

2. _____    6. _____

3. _____    7. _____

4. _____    8. _____

**Word Clues** Write the Spelling Word that fits each clue best.

9. You can use this word when you give a reason.

10. This word isn't a father, but a _____.

11. This word is the first thing you say when you count.

12. You can use this word when you compare two things.

9. _____    11. _____

10. _____    12. _____

Theme 1: **Off to Adventure!**    29

# Proofreading and Writing

**Proofreading** Circle the four misspelled Spelling Words in this postcard. Then write each word correctly on the lines below.

Dear Peter,

I just wanted to send a card to say hi befor I get going again. I fond this one in a little store in Yellowknife. Things are going great, and I'll have a lot of stories to tell when I get home. I'm sorry I havn't written in so long. I'll try to be better about it than I have been. Say hi to Mom and Dad, and tell then I'll call soon.

Love,
Kim

1. _____   3. _____

2. _____   4. _____

**Adventure Dialogue** Get together with another student and write a dialogue about an adventure. Both people in the dialogue can be off adventuring, or you can have one of them stay at home. Use Spelling Words from the list.

Name _____

# Crossword Challenge!

Write the word that matches each clue in the puzzle.
Use the words in the box and your glossary for help.

### Vocabulary

| armor | comrades | endured | farewell |
| triumphant | troops | victorious | |

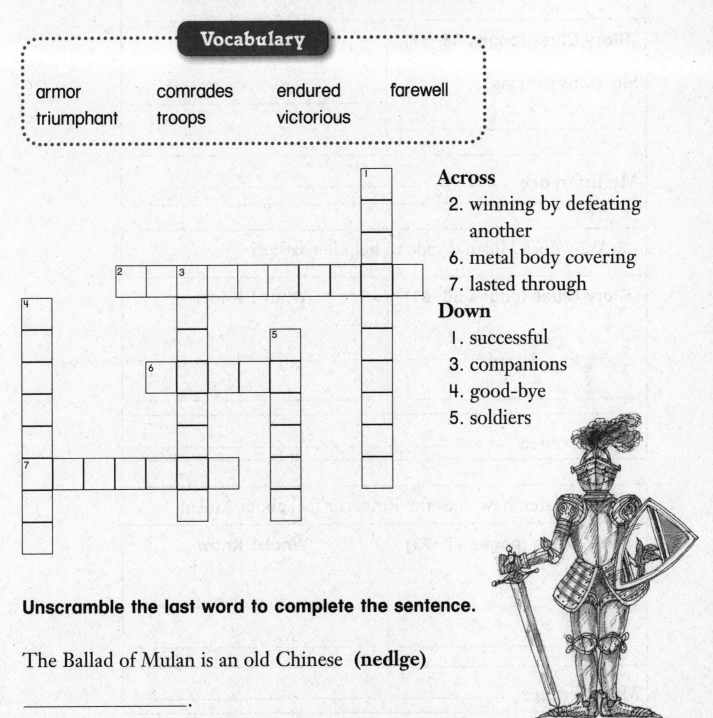

**Across**

2. winning by defeating another
6. metal body covering
7. lasted through

**Down**

1. successful
3. companions
4. good-bye
5. soldiers

**Unscramble the last word to complete the sentence.**

The Ballad of Mulan is an old Chinese  **(nedlge)**

_____.

Name _____

# Inference Chart

| 1. At the beginning of the story, how does Mulan feel? | |
|---|---|
| **Story Clues (pages 56–57)**<br><br>She stops weaving.<br><br>_____ | **What I Know**<br><br><br>_____<br><br>_____ |

**My Inference** _____

| 2. Why does Mulan decide to help her father? | |
|---|---|
| **Story Clues (pages 58–61)**<br><br><br>_____<br><br>_____ | **What I Know**<br><br><br>_____<br><br>_____ |

**My Inference** _____

| 3. Years later, how does the Emperor feel about Mulan? | |
|---|---|
| **Story Clues (pages 72–73)**<br><br><br>_____<br><br>_____ | **What I Know**<br><br><br>_____<br><br>_____ |

**My Inference** _____

Name _____

# Answers About Mulan

**Answer these questions about *The Ballad of Mulan*.**

1. Why does the Emperor need troops?

   _____

   _____

2. Why does Mulan go to war in her father's place?

   _____

   _____

3. After the war, why does the Emperor want to honor Mulan?

   _____

   _____

4. How does Mulan's family feel about having her come home?

   _____

   _____

5. When Mulan returns home, what does she choose to do?

   _____

   _____

6. What is the meaning of Mulan's statement about the rabbits?

   _____

   _____

7. Why do the Chinese still honor Mulan?

   _____

   _____

Name _____

# Make a Good Guess

**Read the story below. Then answer the questions on the following page.**

## The Ice Girl

Trolls were raiding the valley. They swooped down from icy mountain caves, looking for workers and burning houses and barns. Those unlucky enough to be caught never saw daylight again. The people in the valley called a meeting to deal with the problem.

Greta sat and knitted. Ever since Father had fallen, Brother was doing all the family chores. Even at this late hour, he had gone to town while Father slept. Greta helped as best she could. In her spare time, she knitted and knitted. Perhaps her work would help to keep them from selling a cow.

Suddenly, Greta heard a noise outside. Trolls! She slipped out a side door and stood waiting. Sure enough, four ugly trolls peered around the barn. Greta stood still. Slowly the trolls crept closer and closer, but Greta never moved. Finally she felt the steam from their mouths. Then she gathered all her strength and yelled, "Boo!" as loud as she could. The trolls jumped. Then they ran off, as fast as their feet could move. From that day on, no troll ever came back to the valley again.

And to this day, people remember her deed. They have even put up a sign. It reads, "Here is where Greta, the Ice Girl, once lived. She drove the trolls away by saying '*Boo!*'"

Name _____

# Make a Good Guess continued

**Use clues from the story and what you know to answer each question below.**

1. What did the people want to do about the trolls?

_____

_____

2. What happened to people who were caught by the trolls?

_____

_____

3. Why did Brother have to do all the family chores?

_____

_____

4. Why did Greta spend so much time knitting?

_____

_____

5. At the end, why were no trolls ever seen in the valley again?

_____

_____

Name _____

# Syllabication

If you come across a word you can't pronounce, try dividing the word into **syllables**, or parts of a word that are said out loud as single sounds. Each word below has two syllables. Each can be divided in a different way.

**Divide the compound word into two words:**

sunrise = sun • rise

**Divide the word between two consonants:**

village = vil • lage

**Write the words below with spaces between the two syllables. Divide them either between the words in a compound word or between two consonants.**

1. mirror         _____

   _____

2. nightfall      _____

   _____

3. poster         _____

   _____

4. mountain    _____

   _____

5. downtown  _____

   _____

Name _____

# More Short Vowels

A short vowel sound is usually spelled with one vowel followed by a consonant sound.

　　The /ŏ/ sound is usually spelled *o*, as in l**o**t.

　　The /ŭ/ sound is usually spelled *u*, as in r**u**b.

▶ Sometimes the /ŭ/ sound is spelled in a different way. In the starred words *does* and *won*, the /ŭ/ sound is spelled *oe* and *o*.

**Write each Spelling Word under its vowel sound.**

**Spelling Words**

1. pond
2. luck
3. drop
4. lot
5. rub
6. does*
7. drum
8. sock
9. hunt
10. crop
11. shut
12. won*

**/ŏ/ Sound**

_____

_____

_____

_____

_____

**/ŭ/ Sound**

_____

_____

_____

_____

_____

_____

_____

Theme 1: **Off to Adventure!** 　37

Name _____

# Spelling Spree

**Finding Words** Write the Spelling Word hidden in each of these words.

**Spelling Words**

1. pond
2. luck
3. drop
4. lot
5. rub
6. does*
7. drum
8. sock
9. hunt
10. crop
11. shut
12. won*

1. shutter    _____

2. wonderful    _____

3. plot    _____

4. rubber    _____

5. doesn't    _____

6. eardrum    _____

**Questions** Write a Spelling Word to answer each question.

7. What do you wear inside a shoe?

8. What does a farmer grow?

9. What can help you win a game?

10. What body of water is smaller than a lake?

11. What do lions do to get their dinner?

12. What do you call a tiny bead of water?

7. _____    10. _____

8. _____    11. _____

9. _____    12. _____

Name _____

# Proofreading and Writing

**Proofreading** **Circle the five misspelled Spelling Words below. Then write each word correctly.**

### The Emperor Praises Mulan

The Emperor welcomed General Mulan to the High Palace today. First, a soldier played a huge drume. Then the Emperor gave a speech. He told how Mulan was willing to droppe everything to join the army. He said the famous general did not win battles by luk, but by skill and bravery. Now, thanks to Mulan, the war is wone. No longer dose an invading army threaten China. The gates of the Great Wall are safely shut.

**Spelling Words**

1. pond
2. luck
3. drop
4. lot
5. rub
6. does*
7. drum
8. sock
9. hunt
10. crop
11. shut
12. won*

1. _____     4. _____

2. _____     5. _____

3. _____

**Write a Story** Long ago, in a land far away, a brave young girl named Mulan began a dangerous adventure. How would you begin an adventure story? What setting would you use? It could be a dark jungle or a distant planet, or it might be your own neighborhood.

**On a separate sheet of paper, write the opening paragraph of an adventure story. Use Spelling Words from the list.**

Name _____

# Multiple Meaning Words

> **long** *adjective* **1.** Having great length: *a long river.*
> **2.** Lasting for a large amount of time: *a long movie.*
> **3.** Lasting a certain length: *The show was an hour long.*
> ♦ *adverb* Far away in the past: *The dinosaurs lived long ago.*
> ♦ *verb* To wish or want very much: *The children longed for an ice cream cone.*

**For each of the following sentences, choose the correct definition of the underlined word. Write the definition on the line.**

1. <u>Long</u> ago, a girl named Mulan went into battle.

   _____

2. A <u>long</u> line of soldiers crossed the mountain.

   _____

3. The town <u>longed</u> for peace to return.

   _____

4. It was a <u>long</u> way to the Yellow River.

   _____

5. Mulan <u>longed</u> to hear her mother's voice.

   _____

6. The war was ten years <u>long</u>.

   _____

Name _____

# Classifying Sentences

**Read and classify each sentence.  Write *statement*, *question*, *command*, or *exclamation* on the line provided.**

1. Why did Mulan fight in the army? _____

2. What an amazing girl she is! _____

3. Tell me what her journey was like. _____

4. She was surrounded by many dangers. _____

5. Mulan's family and friends were very proud of her.

   _____

6. There she goes now! _____

7. Watch the victory parade. _____

8. Can you see Mulan at the front of the troops?

   _____

9. The musicians sing a song about Mulan's

   adventures. _____

10. How beautiful the music sounds!

   _____

Name _____

# Arranging Sentences

**Arrange these sentences to create an interview with Mulan. Four of the sentences are questions and four are the answers to these questions. On the lines below, write each question followed by its answer. Add the correct end marks.**

| | |
|---|---|
| I dressed in armor | I was terrified at first |
| Were you afraid | Why did you join the army |
| My father was too ill to fight | Look at my face and see how |
| Are you glad to be home |     happy I am |
| | What did you wear |

1. **Q:** _____

   **A:** _____

2. **Q:** _____

   **A:** _____

3. **Q:** _____

   **A:** _____

4. **Q:** _____

   **A:** _____

Name _____

# Capitalizing and Punctuating Sentences

Capital letters and punctuation help us to understand writing. Three students decided to act out a scene from *The Ballad of Mulan*. Here is the script they wrote for the scene. Check the capitalization and punctuation of each sentence. Then rewrite the script, using the correct capitalization and punctuation.

**Soldier 1:** Mulan, is that really you

1. _____

**Soldier 2:** how is this possible

2. _____

**Soldier 1:** are you really a girl

3. _____

**Mulan:** yes, I am you have not seen the real me

4. _____

**Soldier 1:** you are brave and amazing

5. _____

**Soldier 2:** what a remarkable girl you are

6. _____

**Mulan:** I had to save my father would you have let me fight if I had dressed as a woman

7. _____

_____

Name _____

# Response Journal

**Writing a Response Journal Entry** Write about a story you are reading now.  Answer the questions.  Use your own ideas.

**Title of Story** _____

How do I feel about what happens in the story?

_____

_____

How do I feel about the main character?

_____

_____

What do I think will happen next in the story?

_____

_____

What puzzles me about the story?

_____

_____

Which character in the story is most like me? Why?

_____

_____

Name _____

# Capitalizing Days and Months

► Begin an entry in your journal with the day or date.
► Begin the name of the day of the week with a capital letter.

| | | | |
|---|---|---|---|
| **M**onday | **T**uesday | **W**ednesday | **T**hursday |
| **F**riday | **S**aturday | **S**unday | |

► Begin the months of the year with capital letters.

**A**pril 12
**N**ovember 24

**Write each day or date correctly.**

1. wednesday _____

2. friday, november 18 _____

3. saturday _____

4. monday, january 7 _____

5. thursday _____

6. tuesday, may 8 _____

7. sunday _____

Name _____

# What a Day!

**Joey has just moved to a new town. Help him finish a letter to his friend. Fill in the blanks with the correct words from the box.**

**Vocabulary**

rumpled
situations
worried
visible
unusual
directions

September 5

Dear Flora:

My first day of school was full of unlucky

_____. I wanted to wear my favorite

shirt, but it was all _____ from being

packed in a box. While I was looking for something else to

wear, I missed the bus. My parents drove me to school, but we

got lost on the way. We had to stop and ask for

_____. I was _____

that I would be late for school, but we got there just in time.

At noon, I couldn't find my lunchbox. I looked everywhere,

but it wasn't _____. Then my day got

better. Some nice students asked me to sit with them. They

shared their lunches with me. It was an _____ way

to make new friends, but I'm glad it happened!

Your friend,

Joey

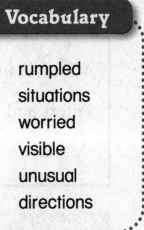

Name _____

# Event Map

**Pages 94–95**

Wendell and Floyd are at the principal's office.  Then Mona

enters and says _____

_____

**Page 96**

Mona leans so far into the bin that only her feet are showing.

A moment later, _____

**Pages 98–99**

The boys _____

**Pages 102**

The children see a sign to the Hat Room, so they follow a

passageway to _____

**Pages 104–106**

The children come to a hallway lined with doors.  Finally, Mona opens

one last door and finds _____

Name _____

# Tell the True Story

**The underlined part of each sentence below is false. Rewrite it as a true sentence about *The Lost and Found*.**

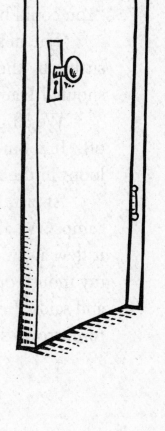

1. Wendell and Floyd are waiting to see the principal because they missed <u>their bus</u>.

   _____

   _____

2. Mona walks into the office to <u>borrow some lunch money</u>.

   _____

   _____

3. The boys want to climb into the Lost and Found bin to <u>get away from a giant squid</u>.

   _____

   _____

4. The children cross the lake to find <u>the school library</u>.

   _____

5. In the Hat Room, the boys start <u>looking for their lost baseball caps</u>.

   _____

6. Mona finds her lucky hat <u>hanging on the Hat Room door</u>.

   _____

Name _____

# Story Events

**Read the story. Think about what happens. Then fill in the chart on the next page.**

## Surprise!

After a long drive, Mom, Dad, and I got to Golden Lake. We were tired, so we set up camp and climbed into our sleeping bags. Then I said, "I hate camping. Why did you make me come?"

"You never know what can happen, Jenny," Dad answered. "You could be in for a big surprise!"

The next morning, I couldn't believe my eyes. There, sitting by the tent was a bee the size of an airplane! "Hop on!" shouted Dad over its loud hum. "Come for a ride."

We all got onto the bee's big, fuzzy back. Then it lifted off. It zoomed right and left. It sailed over the water and made loops in the air. What a fun ride!

At last, the bee landed by our camp. We all climbed off. Then it flew away. I stood there with my mouth open. Dad smiled and said, "Just wait until tomorrow's surprise!"

Name _____

# Story Events  continued

**Fill in the blanks to tell what happened in the story.**

The family sets up camp at Golden Lake.

Jenny says she hates camping, but Dad tells her she may be in for a surprise.

The next morning _____

The family climbs onto its back.

Then the bee _____

At last the bee _____

The family climbs off.

The bee _____

Name _____

# Base Words

Some words are formed from a **base word,** a word that can stand by itself. In the word *climbing,* the base word is *climb.* Letters can be added to the beginning or the end of a base word, as you see here.

appear/**dis**appear      boat/boat**er**      turn/turn**ed**

**Some of the words in this Lost and Found bin contain base words. Circle the base word in those words. Then write each base word on the lines below.**

| asked | unusual | closer | only |
|-------|---------|--------|------|
| principal | trying | nonsense | loosely |

1._____

2._____

3._____

4._____

5._____

6._____

Name _____

# The Vowel-Consonant-*e* Pattern

The long *a, i, o,* and *u* sounds are shown as /ā/, /ī/, /ō/, and /o͞o/. When you hear these sounds, remember that they are often spelled with the vowel-consonant-*e* pattern.

    /ā/ **save**    /ī/ **life**    /ō/ **smoke**    /o͞o/ **huge**

► In the starred words *come* and *love*, the *o*-consonant-*e* pattern spells the /ŭ/ sound.

**Write each Spelling Word under its vowel sound.**

**/ā/ or /ī/ Sound**

_____

_____

_____

_____

**/ō/ or /o͞o/ Sound**

_____

_____

**No long vowel Sound**

_____

_____

Spelling Words

1. smoke
2. huge*
3. save
4. life
5. wide
6. come*
7. mine
8. grade
9. smile
10. note
11. cube
12. love

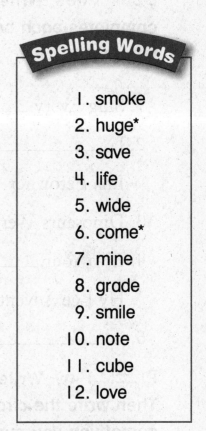

Theme 1: **Off to Adventure!**   53

Name _____

# Spelling Spree

**Book Titles** **Write the Spelling Word that best completes each book title. Remember to use capital letters.**

1. Sing Every _____ by B. A. Soprano

2. I _____ My Cats and Dogs by

   Ima Petowner

3. Dinosaurs Were _____! by Sy N. Tific

4. Live Your _____ to the Fullest by

   Hy Lee Adventurous

5. _____ to My Party by U. R. Invited

**Spelling Words**

1. smoke
2. huge*
3. save
4. life
5. wide
6. come*
7. mine
8. grade
9. smile
10. note
11. cube
12. love

**Puzzle Play** **Write a Spelling Word for each clue. Then write the circled letters in order to spell something you might see over a waterfall.**

6. a year of school ___ ◯ ___ ___ ___

7. to keep for a while ___ ◯ ___ ___

8. a happy expression ___ ___ ◯ ___ ___

9. belongs to me ___ ___ ◯ ___

10. one shape for ice ___ ___ ◯ ___

11. fire can cause it ___ ___ ◯ ___ ___

12. opposite of narrow ◯ ___ ___ ___

___ ___ ___ ___ ___ ___ ___

Name _____

# Proofreading and Writing

**Proofreading** Circle the five misspelled Spelling Words in the sign. Then write each word correctly.

**MY HAT IS LOST!**

Please help me find my hat. I don't know where I left it. The hat is green and has a wid blue ribbon. My mother says it is huje, but I luv it. I'm sure no one else has a hat just like min. If you find it, please leave a not on my locker.

A classmate

## Spelling Words

1. smoke
2. huge*
3. save
4. life
5. wide
6. come*
7. mine
8. grade
9. smile
10. note
11. cube
12. love

1. _____

2. _____

3. _____

4. _____

5. _____

**Write a Description** Have you ever lost something that you liked very much, such as a piece of clothing or a toy?

**On a separate sheet of paper, write a short description of the item you lost. Make sure to include details that would help someone recognize it. Use Spelling Words from the list.**

Name _____

# Entry Words

**Suppose Floyd wrote this letter. Decide whether each underlined word would be an entry word in a dictionary or part of an entry. Write the word in the correct column.**

Dear Ms. Gernsblatt,

   Our visit to the Lost and Found was a real
<u>adventure</u>! First, Wendell and I <u>climbed</u> into the bin to
find Mona. You cannot imagine what happened next. The
bin became a deep well full of lost stuff. Mona was
waiting for us at the bottom. We <u>followed</u> her into a
cave. The cave had a treasure chest, a suit of <u>armor</u>, and a
lot of other old things. We crossed a <u>bubbling</u> lake. We
went through a <u>tunnel</u>. Then we came to a <u>winding</u>
hallway. Finally, we found the Hat Room. You will not
believe this, but Mona's hat was in her <u>purse</u> all along!
After a long time, we found the way back. I think the
three of us are going to be good friends.
                    Your student

| **Entry Word** | **Part of an Entry** |
| --- | --- |
| _____ | _____ |
| _____ | _____ |
| _____ | _____ |
| _____ | _____ |

Name _____

# Finding Sentences

Read each group of words.  Write *sentence* if the words are a complete sentence.  Write *fragment* if the words are not a complete sentence.  Then rewrite each fragment as a complete sentence.  Add a word or words from the box at the bottom of the page.

1. Floyd wanted a hat. _____

_____

2. Examined a suit of armor. _____

_____

3. The rumpled lucky hat. _____

_____

4. Mona looked for her missing hat. _____

_____

5. Floated on the water. _____

_____

6. Flipped a coin. _____

_____

**Word Bank**

| | | |
|---|---|---|
| adventures | disappeared | Floyd |
| Mona | the boat | Wendell |
| worked | | |

Name _____

# Changing Fragments to Sentences

**Use each fragment below in a complete sentence.**

1. Floyd and his friend Wendell

   _____

2. into a lost and found box

   _____

3. loses her lucky hat

   _____

4. looks like a dragon

   _____

5. in the hat room

   _____

6. an exciting adventure in a strange world

   _____

7. decides which cave to explore

   _____

8. a burgundy fez with a small gold tassel

   _____

Name _____

# Finding Sentences

**Effective writers use complete sentences. Correct each sentence fragment. Write your revised sentence on each line. If it is a complete sentence, write the word *correct*.**

## Lucky Hats for Lucky Cats

1. Mona's cat. Likes Mona's lucky hat.

   _____

2. Laughs at the ridiculous cat.

   _____

3. The playful cat. Bites the floppy hat.

   _____

4. Then the cat runs away with the hat.

   _____

5. Chases her cat into the basement.

   _____

6. She hears. A meow.

   _____

7. Mona opens the suitcase.

   _____

8. The cat. Is on her lucky hat.

   _____

Name _____

# Writing a Friendly Letter

The person I will write to: _____

My address: _____

_____

The date: _____

How I will greet the receiver: _____

Why I want to write: _____

_____

The most important thing I want to say: _____

_____

_____

Important details I want to include: _____

_____

_____

How I will close: _____

_____

Name _____

# Using Commas in Dates and Places

► When writing dates, use a comma between the day and the year.   **Example:** May 12, 2003

► Use a comma after the year except at the end of a sentence.

   **Example:** On June 30, 2003, my sister will be ten years old.

► Use a comma between a town or city and the state.

   **Example:** New Orleans, Louisiana

► Use a comma after the state except at the end of a sentence.

   **Example:** My brother goes to college in New Orleans, Louisiana, and we will visit him next month.

**Proofread the letter and add commas where necessary.**

653 Cauterskill Road
Catskills  New York 12414
February 25  2005

Dear Uncle Frank,

    Our class is taking a field trip to New York City.  Mom and Dad are going to be parent helpers.  We want to spend an evening with you.  We take a bus to New York New York  on May 12  2005  and return on the morning of May 14  2005.  Can you let us know right away which date is best for you?  We can't wait to see you in New York New York!

Your nephew,
*Michael*

Name _____

# Radio Words

**Fill each blank with the Key Vocabulary word that
best completes the sentence.**

**Vocabulary**

distress
ferocious
hurricane
raise
relaying
transmitting

1. Jake and Michael couldn't _____
   their friend on the radio.

2. Is the radio _____ a signal?

3. High winds and rain from the

   _____ flooded the town and

   damaged many homes near the ocean.

4. Minutes before the show, the actor still couldn't find his

   costume. He was in great _____.

5. There was a _____ snowstorm in January.

6. Marcus is in the principal's office. He is _____

   a message from his teacher.

**Answer the questions.**

7. Circle the two vocabulary words that have similar meanings.

   relaying       hurricane       distress       transmitting

8. Circle the animal that is the most ferocious.

   goldfish       rabbit       lion       mouse

Name _____

# Cause-and-Effect Chart

**In each box, write a cause or an effect from the
appropriate story.**

## Radio Rescue

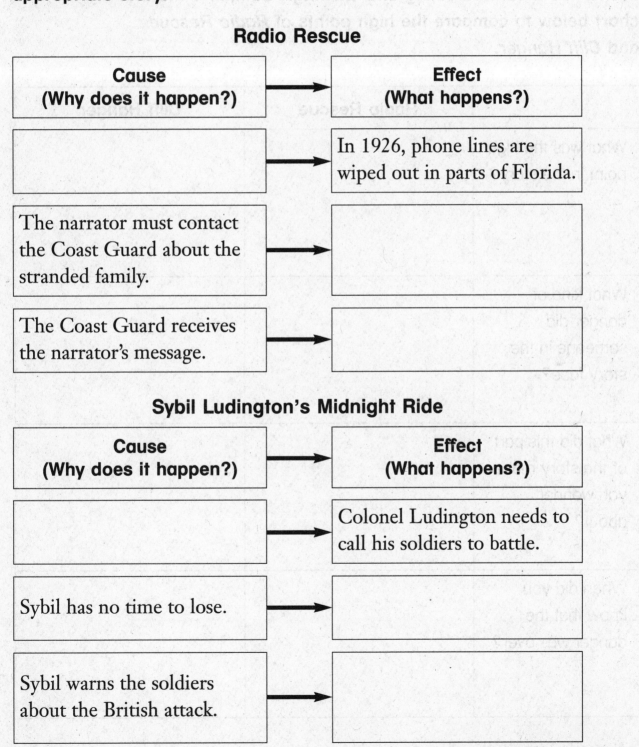

| Cause (Why does it happen?) | Effect (What happens?) |
|---|---|
| | In 1926, phone lines are wiped out in parts of Florida. |
| The narrator must contact the Coast Guard about the stranded family. | |
| The Coast Guard receives the narrator's message. | |

## Sybil Ludington's Midnight Ride

| Cause (Why does it happen?) | Effect (What happens?) |
|---|---|
| | Colonel Ludington needs to call his soldiers to battle. |
| Sybil has no time to lose. | |
| Sybil warns the soldiers about the British attack. | |

Theme 1: **Off to Adventure!**   63

Name _____

# The High Point

The high point of a story is the point at which the story's events are most interesting and exciting. Complete the chart below to compare the high points of *Radio Rescue* and *Cliff Hanger*.

| | Radio Rescue | Cliff Hanger |
|---|---|---|
| What was the high point in the story? | | |
| What kind of danger did someone in the story face? | | |
| What did this part of the story make you wonder about? | | |
| When did you know that the danger was over? | | |

Name _____

# Riders Beware!

**Carousel is a friendly horse but there are certain things that upset him. Help the stable manager complete a sign that explains to riders how to keep Carousel happy.**

### Vocabulary

| reins | route | trot | urged |

My name is Carousel. I have lived at Sunshine Stables for over 15 years. I know each _____ through the woods around here.

If you ride with me, you are in for a treat!

I like giving rides to people. I am usually very friendly, but some things make me unfriendly.

I get angry when riders pull hard on my _____. It hurts my mouth.

I get mad when I am _____ to go fast. I don't mind speeding up to a _____ now and then, but I will not run!

If you follow my rules, I am sure we will get along very well.

Name _____

# Test Practice

**Use the three steps you've learned to choose the best answer for these questions about *Sybil Ludington's Midnight Ride*. Fill in the circle next to the best answer.**

1. Why does Sybil ride at night to the farms nearby?

   ◯ She needs to tell the soldiers to gather at her father's farm.

   ◯ She hopes to find shelter.

   ◯ She wants to tell her father that the British are coming.

   ◯ She must tell the soldiers to burn the town of Danbury.

2. Why did the author write this story?

   ◯ to tell a story about an important event in history

   ◯ to persuade readers to buy a horse like Star

   ◯ to explain how to deliver an important message

   ◯ to describe Sybil's childhood

3. Where does the story take place?

   ◯ in Great Britain          ◯ on a farm

   ◯ at Sybil's school          ◯ in Connecticut

4. **Connecting/Comparing** How is Sybil like Mulan in *The Ballad of Mulan?*

   ◯ She travels to faraway lands.

   ◯ She misses her parents.

   ◯ She is brave during a war.

   ◯ She hopes to become a general.

*Continue on page 67.*

# Test Practice continued

5. What is another good title for this story?

   ○ Fires at Night

   ○ Warning Soldiers

   ○ A Cold, Wet Ride

   ○ Sybil and Star

6. Why are the soldiers at their farms instead of with Colonel Ludington?

   ○ They have decided not to fight the British.

   ○ They have gone home to plant their crops.

   ○ They are hiding from the British.

   ○ They are gathering supplies for the fight.

7. How does Sybil probably feel when she hears the bell in Carmel?

   ○ calm             ○ upset

   ○ worried          ○ hopeful

8. **Connecting/Comparing** How are Sybil's actions similar to the boy's actions in *Radio Rescue?*

   ○ She carefully writes down different names.

   ○ She helps spread the word about an emergency.

   ○ She knows how to use a ham radio.

   ○ She tells family members that their loved ones are safe.

**Monitoring Student Progress**

Comprehension Skill Cause and Effect

# What Happened?  Why?

**Read the information in the chart below.  Then fill in the blanks to complete the chart.  Look back at the Anthology pages listed if you want to check the details of an event.**

| Cause (Why did it happen?) | Effect (What happened?) |
|---|---|
| _____ _____ _____ | Sybil stayed at each house just long enough to call out her message and listen for an answer. (page 132) |
| A cold rain was falling. (page 133) | _____ _____ _____ |
| Sybil saw fires burning in Danbury. (page 133) | _____ _____ _____ |
| _____ _____ | Sybil did not knock on every door. (page 134) |
| _____ _____ | The American soldiers surprised the British and forced them back to their ships. (page 134) |

Name _____

# When Did It Happen?

**Read the paragraph.**

Juana's clock radio turned on at 7 A.M. Juana groaned and rolled over, trying her best to ignore the radio announcer. A few minutes later, the announcer reported that a fire was burning at First and Main. First and Main? That was less than a block from Juana's house! Within seconds, Juana was out of bed, dressed, and looking out her window. She could see thick black smoke pouring from a window in Ms. Jaramelo's house. Juana scanned the street nervously. Just then, she spotted Ms. Jaramelo, safe and sound on the other side of the street. Moments later, Juana heard the sound of fire engine sirens.

**Read the chart and fill in the blanks.**

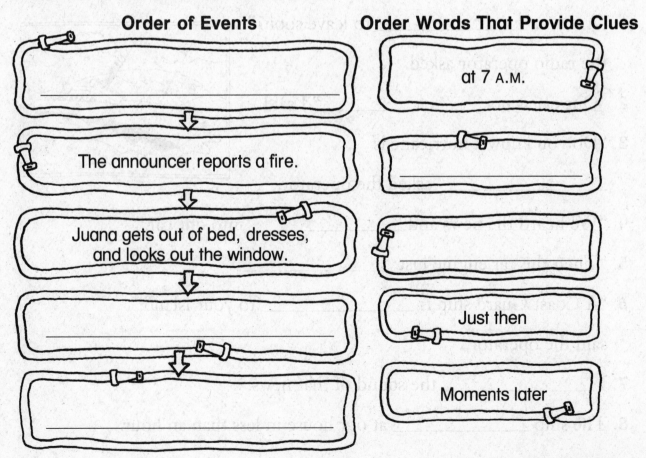

| Order of Events | Order Words That Provide Clues |
|---|---|
| _____ | at 7 A.M. |
| The announcer reports a fire. | _____ |
| Juana gets out of bed, dresses, and <u>looks out</u> the window. | _____ |
| _____ | Just then |
| _____ | Moments later |

Name _____

# Add an Ending

**Complete each sentence with a word from the box.  Use each word one time.  Add *-ed* or *-ing* to the word so it makes sense in the sentence.**

Remember:

• When a word ends in *e*, drop the *e* before adding *-ed* or *-ing*.
• When a word ends with a vowel and a consonant, double the consonant before adding *-ed* or *-ing*.

### Word Bank

| plan | come | hop | sail |
|------|------|-----|------|
| arrive | like | run | stop |

1. "Are you _____ to leave soon?"

   the radio operator asked.

2. "Our car is not _____," I said.

3. "Do you know a hurricane is

   _____?" asked the operator.

4. "We heard the news and _____ into our car."

5. "Then the car engine just _____."

6. "A Coast Guard ship is _____ to your island,"

   said the operator.

7. I _____ the sound of that news.

8. The ship _____ at our house in less than an hour.

# Look for the Right Meaning

**look** *verb* **1.** To use the eyes to see: *I looked at the picture.* **2.** To focus one's gaze or attention: *Please look at the camera.* **3.** To appear; seem: *These bananas look ripe.* **4.** To search: *I looked everywhere for the missing key.* ♦ *noun* **1.** An act of looking: *I took a quick look at my watch.* **2.** An expression, as on a person's face: *She had a friendly look on her face.*

**Read each sentence. Choose the correct definition of the underlined word. Write the definition on the line.**

1. Dad and I <u>looked</u> for our binoculars.

_____

2. We wanted to <u>look</u> at the stars at night.

_____

3. The night sky <u>looks</u> so mysterious to me.

_____

4. I took a <u>look</u> through the binoculars.

_____

5. When I saw them close up, the stars <u>looked</u> brighter.

_____

6. Dad said my face had an amazed <u>look</u>.

_____

Name _____

# Spelling Review

**Write Spelling Words from the list to answer the questions.**

1–17. Which seventeen words have short vowels?

1. _____        10. _____

2. _____        11. _____

3. _____        12. _____

4. _____        13. _____

5. _____        14. _____

6. _____        15. _____

7. _____        16. _____

8. _____        17. _____

9. _____

18–25. Which eight words have the vowel-consonant-*e* pattern?

18. _____        22. _____

19. _____        23. _____

20. _____        24. _____

21. _____        25. _____

**Spelling Words**

1. drum
2. huge
3. last
4. drop
5. class
6. left
7. wide
8. mix
9. send
10. save
11. smell
12. stick
13. note
14. thick
15. hunt
16. thin
17. grade
18. lot
19. cube
20. pond
21. life
22. sock
23. luck
24. shut
25. smile

Name _____

# Spelling Spree

**Book Titles** Write the Spelling Word that best completes each funny book title. Remember to use capital letters.

**Spelling Words**

1. class
2. mix
3. send
4. smell
5. stick
6. pond
7. sock
8. drum
9. huge
10. grade
11. cube
12. smile

Example: *The Great _____ from Planet X*
by I. C. Starrs ___Escape___

1. *Put an Ice _____ in My Glass and Other Science Experiments* by Sy N. Seen

2. *A _____ Is a Frown Upside Down* by Mary Timz

3. *My First Day in _____ 3: A True Story* by Ima Newcomer

4. *The Mystery in the Third Grade _____* by Minnie Klooz

5. *_____ Us a Post Card* by U. R. A. Riter

6. *Do I _____ Cookies?* by I. M. Hungree

1. _____  4. _____

2. _____  5. _____

3. _____  6. _____

**One, Two, Three!** Write the Spelling Word that belongs in each group.

7. piano, guitar, _____  10. stir, blend, _____

8. big, large, _____  11. shirt, shoe, _____

9. lake, river, _____  12. twig, branch, _____

# Proofreading and Writing

**Proofreading** Circle the five misspelled Spelling Words below. Then write each word correctly.

**Spelling Words**

1. lot
2. left
3. thick
4. life
5. thin
6. last
7. luck
8. note
9. class
10. hunt
11. drop
12. wide
13. save
14. shut

January 12—Today I went on a treasure hunte. I spent a lott of time looking for the treasure in a thic grove of trees and near the pond. I didn't have any luk. Maybe somebody will drap a clue that I will find!

1. _____    4. _____

2. _____    5. _____

3. _____

**A Newspaper Article** Write a Spelling Word that means the same as each underlined word or words.

Jeremy is a 6. <u>skinny</u> boy in Mr. Boyd's third grade 7. <u>group</u>. All of his 8. <u>years of being</u> Jeremy had heard about a buried treasure. One day he found a 9. <u>short letter</u> in his attic. It was all that was 10. <u>still around</u> of his grandfather's things. He 11. <u>closed</u> the door and read. "Keep your eyes 12. <u>all the way</u> open," it said. "Look under the 13. <u>final</u> tree in the yard." There Jeremy found a journal that he will 14. <u>keep</u>.

6. _____   9. _____   12. _____

7. _____   10. _____   13. _____

8. _____   11. _____   14. _____

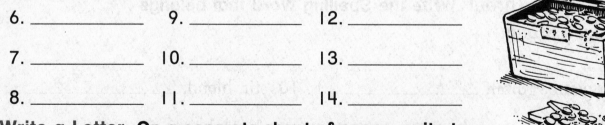

**Write a Letter** On a separate sheet of paper, write to a friend about a buried treasure you hope to find. Use the Spelling Review Words.

Name _____

# Finding Sentences

**Read each group of words. Write *sentence* if the words are a complete sentence. Write *fragment* if the words are not a complete sentence. Then rewrite each fragment as a complete sentence.**

1. The boy listens to messages. _____

   _____

2. Hears about a family in trouble. _____

   _____

3. Stranded on an island. _____

   _____

4. He uses the emergency channel. _____

   _____

5. Sends a message to the U.S. Coast Guard. _____

   _____

6. The family has been saved! _____

   _____

Name _____

# Listing Subjects and Predicates

**Write the complete subject of each sentence in the Subjects column. Write the complete predicate of each sentence in the Predicates column.**

1. A young girl mounted her horse.

2. Rain fell from the sky.

3. The girl rode to a nearby farm.

4. She banged on the door.

5. A sleepy farmer opened the door.

6. The young rider shouted the news.

| **Subjects** | **Predicates** |
| --- | --- |
| _____ | _____ |
| _____ | _____ |
| _____ | _____ |
| _____ | _____ |
| _____ | _____ |
| _____ | _____ |

Name _____

# Poetry Words

**Choose the word from the box that best completes each sentence. Then circle each word in the puzzle below.**

1. *Night, write,* and *sight* are words that

   _____.

2. The first two _____ of my poem have six

   words each.

3. I counted the _____ in every line.

4. The _____ of the rhymes is that every pair of

   lines rhyme.

5. My poem is divided into four _____. Each

   one has four lines.

6. My poem has a gentle, steady _____.

| R | H | Y | M | L | P | L | P | S | B |
|---|---|---|---|---|---|---|---|---|---|
| H | E | S | B | I | B | I | A | T | R |
| Y | S | T | E | N | E | N | T | A | H |
| T | R | P | A | T | T | E | R | N | Y |
| H | H | S | T | A | N | S | H | Z | M |
| M | Y | P | S | T | A | N | R | A | S |
| P | A | T | R | H | Y | M | E | S | L |

Name _____

# Patterns of Poetry

## Poems with Rhyme Words

| Poem | Poem | Poem |
|---|---|---|
| _____ | _____ | _____ |
| **Pairs of Rhyme Words** | **Pairs of Rhyme Words** | **Pairs of Rhyme Words** |
| | | |

## Poems with Repeated Words

| Poem | Poem | Poem |
|---|---|---|
| _____ | _____ | _____ |
| **Examples of Repeated Words** | **Examples of Repeated Words** | **Examples of Repeated Words** |
| | | |

## Poems with Different Line Patterns

| Poems with Very Short Lines | Poems Written in Stanzas | Poems with Lines That Form a Shape |
|---|---|---|
| | | |

Name _____

# Comparing Poems

**Think about the elements of poetry.  Choose three poems to compare and contrast.  Then complete the chart below.**

| | Title: _____ | Title: _____ | Title: _____ |
|---|---|---|---|
| What picture does the poem create in your mind? | | | |
| What feeling does the poem express? | | | |
| What kind of language is used in each poem? | | | |

Tell which of these poems is your favorite and why.

_____

_____

_____

Name _____

# And the Winner Is ....

**You are presenting the annual Poetry Prizes. Below are the notes for your speech. Use the poems from this theme to fill in the blanks.**

POETRY
PRIZE

### Best Rhyme

The poem with the Best Rhyme is _____.

The winning rhyming words are _____

and _____.

Other good rhyming words in the poem are

_____ _____.

### Best Rhythm

The poem with the Best Rhythm is _____.

A line I like from the poem is _____

_____.

### Best Words That Paint a Picture

The poem with the Best Words That Paint a Picture

is _____.

My favorite lines from the poem are _____

_____

_____.

Name _____

# Tell About a Poem

**Choose another poem to study closely.  Make notes about rhyme words, images, and repetition on the chart.  Then write a paragraph that describes how the poem uses each of these elements.  Use examples to support your ideas.**

**Poem:** _____

| | |
|---|---|
| Rhyme Words | |
| Images | |
| Repetition | |

_____

_____

_____

_____

_____

_____

**Focus on Poetry**

Structural Analysis  Prefixes
*un-*, *dis-*, and *non-;* Suffixes
*-y* and *-ly*

# Good Muffin, Healthy Muffin

Some words combine a prefix and a base word.

    un- + true  untrue

    dis- + appear  disappear

    non- + stop  nonstop

Other words combine a base word and a suffix.

    mess + -y  messy

    slow + -ly  slowly

Some words combine a prefix, a base word, and a suffix.

    un- + fair + -ly   unfairly

**Read this poem.  Circle each word that has a prefix or suffix
shown in the chart.  Write each word and its base word to
complete the chart.**

I buy a nonfat muffin.
It looks sugary and sweet.
And when I quickly take a bite,
I find that it's a treat!

I don't dislike my muffin
Although I thought I would.
It's not at all unpleasant,
It's healthy and it's good!

| Word with Prefix or Suffix | Base Word |
|---|---|
| un- _____ | _____ |
| _____ | _____ |
| dis- _____ | _____ |
| _____ | _____ |
| non- _____ | _____ |
| _____ | _____ |
| -y _____ | _____ |
| _____ | _____ |
| -ly _____ | _____ |
| _____ | _____ |

Name _____

# More Short and Long Vowels

A short vowel sound is often spelled with one vowel followed by a consonant sound.

st**a**nd          tw**i**st

A long vowel sound is often spelled vowel-consonant-e.

pl**ate**          wh**ite**

**Write each Spelling Word under the heading that describes its vowel sound.**

1. stand
2. rest
3. plate
4. clock
5. white
6. stuff
7. spoke
8. bend
9. frame
10. twist
11. June
12. mile

| Short Vowel Sound | Long Vowel Sound |
| --- | --- |
| _____ | _____ |
| _____ | _____ |
| _____ | _____ |
| _____ | _____ |
| _____ | _____ |
| _____ | _____ |

Name _____

# Spelling Spree

**Rhyme Time** Fill in the blank in each sentence with a
Spelling Word that rhymes with the underlined word.

1. The strong man could _____ on one

   <u>hand</u>.

2. Did you _____ your <u>wrist</u> when you

   fell down?

3. That <u>block</u> is painted to look like a

   _____.

4. Mia's new <u>kite</u> looks like a _____ bird.

5. When Dan _____, he told a funny <u>joke</u>.

6. To do well on the <u>test</u>, you need plenty of

   _____.

**Spelling Words**

1. stand
2. rest
3. plate
4. clock
5. white
6. stuff
7. spoke
8. bend
9. frame
10. twist
11. June
12. mile

**Letter Swap** Change the underlined letter in each word to
make a Spelling Word. Then write the Spelling Word.

7. mi<u>n</u>e _____     10. <u>t</u>une _____

8. <u>m</u>end _____     11. fl<u>a</u>me _____

9. plan<u>e</u> _____     12. st<u>i</u>ff _____

Name _____

# Proofreading and Writing

**Proofreading** **Circle the four misspelled Spelling
Words in this poem.  Then write each word correctly.**

**The Puppy**

A snowball of fur,

So soft and whit,

Blankets my playmate,

Curled up tight

In my lap

At rest.

But if I spok

Or tried to stand,

She'd tiwst and bende,

Nose my hand,

All ready

To play.

1. stand
2. rest
3. plate
4. clock
5. white
6. stuff
7. spoke
8. bend
9. frame
10. twist
11. June
12. mile

1. _____

2. _____

3. _____

4. _____

**Write a Poem About an Animal**  Do you have a pet or a
favorite animal?  What does it look like?  How does it act?
Why do you love or like it?

**On a separate piece of paper, write a poem about a pet or
your favorite animal.  Use Spelling Words from the list.**

Name _____

# Use Your Senses

**Each sentence below uses sensory language. After each sentence, write which of the five senses the description appeals to: *sight, hearing, touch, taste,* or *smell.***

1. The tiny kitten was as <u>soft as a dandelion</u> in the palm of my hand. _____

2. His long fur was as <u>golden as autumn leaves.</u>

   _____

3. He licked my arm with his <u>sandpaper-rough tongue.</u>

   _____

4. I noticed his <u>sweet, slightly fishy breath</u> as he purred in my face.

   _____

5. "What a sweet kitty!" I said in a <u>syrupy voice.</u> _____

6. I was startled when his <u>knife-sharp claws</u> sank into my arm.

   _____

7. I let out an <u>ear-piercing scream</u> and ran out of the room. _____

8. A glass of <u>refreshingly cold water</u> calmed me down.

   _____

9. When I went back into the living room, the kitten gazed at me with his <u>sorrowful emerald eyes.</u>

   _____

10. I said, "Oh, okay, I forgive you," and I poured him a bowl of <u>rich, delicious cream.</u>

Name _____

# Matching Sentence Parts

**Choose a subject or a predicate from the lists below to
complete each fragment. Write the complete sentence on
the line. Some subjects and predicates will not be used.**

| Subjects | Predicates |
|---|---|
| the tall giraffe | hung upside down |
| spaghetti with sauce | curled their tails |
| the shimmering blue sky | ran across the picnic table |
| Andre | gobbled his dinner |
| the birds on the feeder | beat upon my head |

1. Is delicious to eat.

_____

2. The April rain

_____

3. Dreamed about his parents.

_____

4. Walked around on wooden stilts.

_____

5. The batty bat.

_____

6. Tiny red ants.

_____

Name _____

# Correcting Fragments

**Read the paragraph.  Correct each sentence fragment, and
write the revised paragraph below.**

I wrote.  A funny poem.  It told about a silly dragon.
The dragon.  Sneezed.  A lot.  One sneeze made a house
fall down.  One made a tree crash.  Into a pond.  The
poor dragon felt sad.  He asked a friendly dog. For help.
The dog gave this advice.  He told the dragon to eat his
food.  With less pepper.  The dragon's problem.  Went away.
Now he sneezed.  A lot less. And felt better.

_____

_____

_____

_____

_____

Name _____

# Sentence Punctuation and Capitalization

**Use proofreading marks to correct six missing or incorrect end marks and four missing capital letters in this paragraph from a poet's writing diary.**

**Example:**

the songs of the birds woke me at five o'clock today

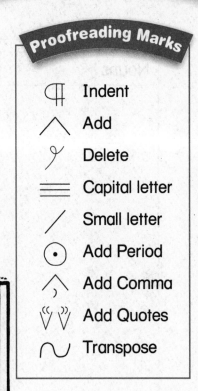

Saturday

    what a wonderful morning it is. My sister and I took a long walk in the park. my sister found a baby bird on the ground We sat and watched it? the bird stayed very still. At last it shook its feathers and flew away?  did its tiny wings carry it to a safe place. I must write a poem about this beautiful little bird

Name _____

# Writing a Shape Poem

Topic _____

| Nouns | Verbs | The Five Senses |
|---|---|---|
| | | |

## Organizing the Words in a Shape

Name _____

# Cool Cat Nouns

Help this poet who wants to write a shape poem about a
cat.  Find six exact **nouns** that tell about cats.  Write them
on the lines below.

| | | | |
|---|---|---|---|
| old | run | soft | hand |
| paw | tail | claw | nose |
| bark | silly | whiskers | happy |
| fur | elephant | sleepy | fork |

Exact Nouns

1. _____

2. _____

3. _____

4. _____

5. _____

6. _____

Name _____

# Celebrating Traditions

**Describe a tradition that you celebrate. When do you celebrate it? Who shares the celebration with you? What is your favorite part of this tradition?**

○ _____
_____
_____
_____
_____
○ _____
_____
_____

**List any traditions you would like to learn about.**

○ _____
_____
_____
_____

Name _____

# Celebrating Traditions

**Fill in the chart as you read the stories.**

**The Keeping Quilt**

What tradition is celebrated in this selection?

Why is this tradition important to those who celebrate it?

**Grandma's Records**

What tradition is celebrated in this selection?

Why is this tradition important to those who celebrate it?

**The Talking Cloth**

What tradition is celebrated in this selection?

Why is this tradition important to those who celebrate it?

**Dancing Rainbows**

What tradition is celebrated in this selection?

Why is this tradition important to those who celebrate it?

Name _____

# Quilt Crossword

Write the word that matches each clue in the puzzle. Use the vocabulary words for help.

**Vocabulary**

border
gathering
needles
scraps
sewn
threaded

**Across**

4. edge

6. tools for sewing

**Down**

1. coming together

2. leftover pieces

3. passed through the eye of a needle

5. put together with a needle and thread

Name _____

# Author's Family Chart

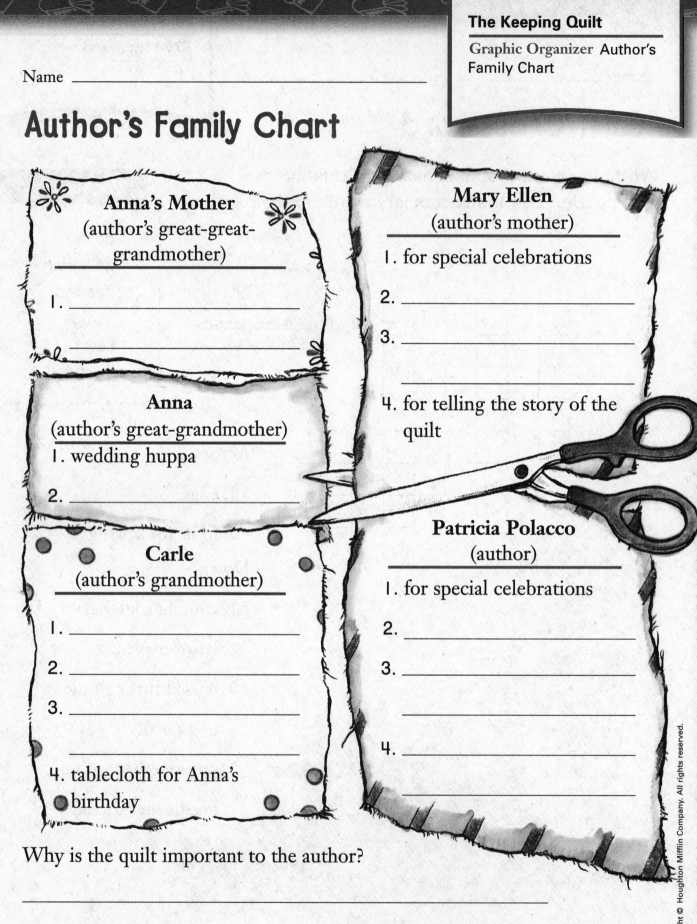

**Anna's Mother**
(author's great-great-grandmother)
_____

1. _____

2. _____

**Anna**
(author's great-grandmother)
1. wedding huppa

2. _____

**Carle**
(author's grandmother)
_____

1. _____

2. _____

3. _____

_____

4. tablecloth for Anna's birthday

**Mary Ellen**
(author's mother)

1. for special celebrations

2. _____

3. _____

_____

4. for telling the story of the quilt

**Patricia Polacco**
(author)
_____

1. for special celebrations

2. _____

3. _____

_____

4. _____

Why is the quilt important to the author?

_____

_____

Name _____

# Piece It Together

**Finish each statement with details from *The Keeping Quilt*.**

1. Anna's mother decides to make the quilt because

_____

_____

2. When Carle grows up, Great-Gramma Anna passes
   the quilt on to her.  She

_____

_____

3. Over the years, people in the family use the quilt as

_____

_____

4. Mary Ellen tells her daughter (the author) whose

_____

_____

5. Mary Ellen also is lucky enough to tell the story of the quilt to

_____

_____

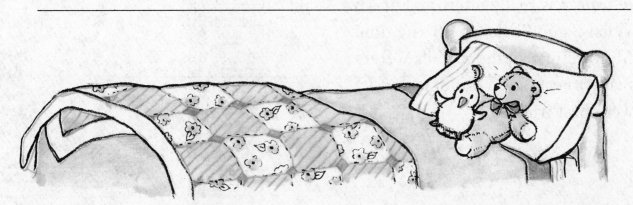

Name _____

# An Author's View

**Read the story. Then finish the chart on the next page.**

## Foxtails

When I first saw Grandma Sorensen in her doorway, she seemed ten feet tall and skinny! She frowned as she squinted into the sun and watched our car. Would I like her?

In the living room, Grandma Sorensen gave each of us a big hug. Then she and Mom began talking. Soon they were laughing about things Mom did as a girl. Once she fell out of their apple tree and broke her arm. Then Grandma told how she too had fallen out of an apple tree and broken her arm. That was when she was a girl in Denmark. I said, "I'm never going to climb apple trees!" Grandma laughed.

Later, after Mom had left for a meeting, Grandma suggested that we make my mother a treat, the one she loved best at my age. In the kitchen, Grandma let me mix flour, sugar, eggs, butter, and vanilla together to make a stiff dough. Then she showed me how to pinch off a small piece of dough, roll it, and twist it into a "foxtail." She didn't mind that I made the tails a bit crooked.

As we worked, Grandma asked me about school and what I wanted to be when I grew up. From her questions I could tell she was really interested in what I said. What a good listener! By the time Mom returned, the foxtails were ready to eat, and Grandma and I were best friends.

# An Author's View continued

Use story details to finish this chart. Tell how the author feels about her grandmother.

| Scene | Details About Grandma | Author's Feelings About Grandma |
|---|---|---|
| **The Doorway** | 1. _____ <br><br> _____ <br><br> 2. _____ <br><br> _____ | _____ <br><br> _____ <br><br> _____ <br><br> _____ |
| **The Living Room** | 1. _____ <br><br> _____ <br><br> 2. _____ | _____ <br><br> _____ <br><br> _____ |
| **The Kitchen** | 1. _____ <br><br> _____ <br><br> 2. _____ <br><br> _____ | _____ <br><br> _____ <br><br> _____ <br><br> _____ |

If you met Grandma Sorensen, do you think you would like her? Why or why not? Use complete sentences.

_____

_____

_____

Name _____

# Compound Mix-up

**Write a compound word to match each picture clue.**
**Each word is made up of two words from the Word Bank.**

**Word Bank**

| dog | bug | pot | lady | flower | flag |
| fly | dragon | tooth | rain | fish | bow |
| house | brush | pole | moon | star | light |

_____   _____   _____

_____   _____   _____

_____   _____   _____

**Combine two words from the Word Bank to make a new compound word.**

_____

Name _____

# More Long Vowel Spellings

To spell a word with the /ā/ sound, remember that /ā/ can be spelled *ai* or *ay*. To spell a word with the /ē/ sound, remember that /ē/ can be spelled *ea* or *ee*.

| /ā/ | ai, ay | p**ai**nt, cl**ay** |
| /ē/ | ea, ee | l**ea**ve, f**ee**l |

► In the starred words *neighbor*, *eight*, and *weigh*, the /ā/ sound is spelled *eigh*.

**Write each Spelling Word under its vowel sound.**

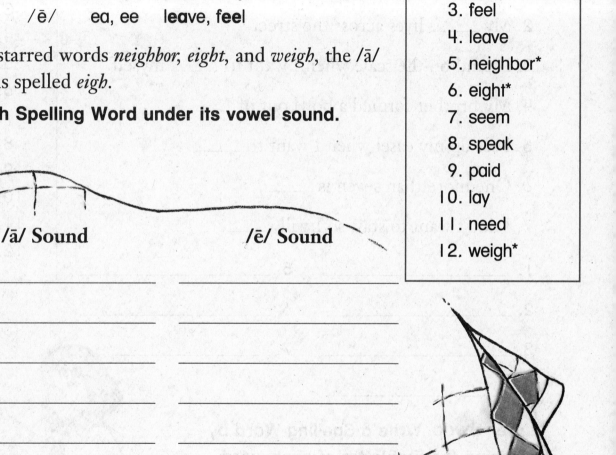

**/ā/ Sound**                    **/ē/ Sound**

_____     _____

_____     _____

_____     _____

_____     _____

_____     _____

_____

Spelling Words

1. paint
2. clay
3. feel
4. leave
5. neighbor*
6. eight*
7. seem
8. speak
9. paid
10. lay
11. need
12. weigh*

Name _____

# Spelling Spree

**Fill in the Blank** Write the Spelling Word that best completes each sentence.

1. I whisper when I need to _____ softly.

2. My _____ lives across the street.

3. I stand on the scale when I want to _____ myself.

4. My brother formed a bowl out of _____.

5. I set up my easel when I want to _____.

6. One more than seven is _____.

7. I don't want to stay, so I will _____.

1. _____    5. _____

2. _____    6. _____

3. _____    7. _____

4. _____

**Spelling Words**

1. paint
2. clay
3. feel
4. leave
5. neighbor*
6. eight*
7. seem
8. speak
9. paid
10. lay
11. need
12. weigh*

**Letter Swap** Write a Spelling Word by changing the first letter of each word.

8. peel _____

9. maid _____

10. seed _____

11. say _____

12. teem _____

Name _____

# Proofreading and Writing

**Proofreading** Circle the five misspelled Spelling Words in this invitation. Then write each word correctly.

Dear New Neighbor,

Please join me and some of the other tenants in the building for a quilting party. I have enough needles and thread for eaght helpers. You don't ned to be a sewing expert. The work will seam easy, and we will all get to know one another. Later we will have tea and cake. The party will be in my apartment next Monday evening. If you are interested, spek to me soon. If you prefer, you can leve a note in my mailbox instead.

Sincerely,
Natasha Pushkin

## Spelling Words

1. paint
2. clay
3. feel
4. leave
5. neighbor*
6. eight*
7. seem
8. speak
9. paid
10. lay
11. need
12. weigh*

1. _____    4. _____

2. _____    5. _____

3. _____

**Write a Description** If you were going to design a quilt like the one in the story, what would it look like?

**On a separate sheet of paper, write about a quilt you would design. Tell what material you would use and why. Use Spelling Words from the list.**

Name _____

# Word Family Reunion

Select the words that belong to the word family for "back."
Then arrange the words on the chart and define each one.
Check your work in a dictionary.

## Word Bank

| | | | | |
|---|---|---|---|---|
| backward | bacteria | backyard | bachelor | backboard |
| backbone | backfire | background | backpack | backup |

## The Back Family

| Word | Meaning |
|---|---|
| 1. _____ | _____ |
| 2. _____ | _____ |
| 3. _____ | _____ |
| 4. _____ | _____ |
| 5. _____ | _____ |
| 6. _____ | _____ |
| 7. _____ | _____ |
| 8. _____ | _____ |

104    Theme 2: **Celebrating Traditions**

Name _____

# In Search of Common Nouns

**Circle the common noun or nouns in each group of words.**

1. big    room

2. quilt    sewed    needle

3. house    talk    enjoy    people

4. blanket    warm    sister    friend

5. happy    silly    story    angry

6. curious    city    cheerful    sad

**Write the circled nouns in the correct square below.**

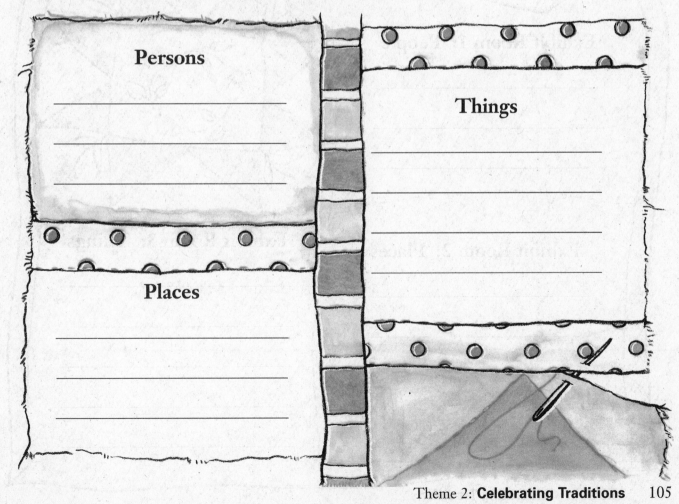

**Persons**

_____

_____

_____

**Places**

_____

_____

**Things**

_____

_____

_____

Theme 2: **Celebrating Traditions**    105

Name _____

# Common Nouns in Signs

**Find the common nouns in the report. Write each common noun in the correct exhibit room below.**

## A Visit to the Museum

My friends and I visited a museum. There we saw a collection of wonderful old quilts. Some of them were made by pioneers. Many of the blankets showed children, flowers, and trees. One showed all fifty states.

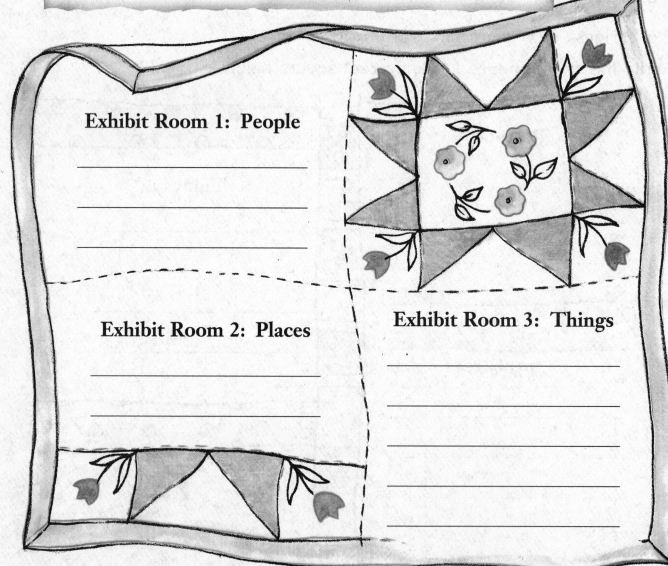

**Exhibit Room 1: People**

_____

_____

_____

**Exhibit Room 2: Places**

_____

_____

**Exhibit Room 3: Things**

_____

_____

_____

_____

Name _____

# Commas in a Series

**Proofread each sentence. Add commas to separate each series of three or more words. Remove all unnecessary commas.**

1. Our attic is filled with boxes bags and books.

   _____

2. I found my great-grandfather's hat gloves and cane.

   _____

3. The cane was carved with tigers lions and elephants.

   _____

4. I also found old journals photographs and drawings.

   _____

5. One photograph shows my aunt uncle and cousin.

   _____

6. My great-grandmother lived on a farm with chickens cows horses and pigs.

   _____

   _____

7. In her diary, she described her, friends relatives and visitors.

   _____

8. Her hopes wishes and dreams, bring every page to life.

   _____

Name _____

# Paragraphs That Compare and Contrast

Use the chart on this page to help you plan paragraphs that compare and contrast. Write what the paragraphs will be about. Write two or three interesting details that show how the people, places, and things are alike. Then write how they are different. Use the details you record in your writing.

## What I Will Compare and Contrast

_____

_____

| How They Are Alike | How They Are Different |
|---|---|
| 1. _____ | 1. _____ |
| _____ | _____ |
| 2. _____ | 2. _____ |
| _____ | _____ |
| 3. _____ | 3. _____ |
| _____ | _____ |

Write your paragraphs that compare and contrast on a separate sheet of paper. Include the details you wrote above.

Name _____

# Sentence Combining

► Connect two related sentences with a comma and
a joining word to make a compound sentence.

► Use a comma and the word *and* to create a
compound sentence that makes a comparison.

**Example:** The gifts were part of the women's bouquets, **and**
each gift was a symbol of something important for a good life.

► Use a comma and the word *but* to create a compound
sentence that makes a contrast.

**Example:** At the first weddings, the women wore
wedding dresses, **but** later some women wore suits.

**Write a compound sentence. Combine the sentences
with a comma and the joining word in parentheses ( ).**

1. The women loved the keeping quilt. They used it to keep
   their family's traditions alive. (and)

   _____

   _____

2. The women's weddings were alike in some ways. They were
   also different. (but)

   _____

   _____

3. The quilt was used as a cape. It was used as a huppa too. (and)

   _____

# Revising Your Instructions

**Reread your instructions. Put a checkmark in the box for each sentence that describes your paper. Use this page to help you revise.**

### Rings the Bell

☐ An interesting beginning tells my topic.

☐ I included all the necessary materials, steps, and details.

☐ The steps are told in order, using time-order words.

☐ I used many exact words. My writing sounds interesting.

☐ Sentences flow well. There are no mistakes.

### Getting Stronger

☐ The beginning tells about my topic but isn't interesting.

☐ I forgot a step or some materials. More details are needed.

☐ A step might be out of order. I used few time-order words.

☐ More exact words are needed. My voice could be stronger.

☐ Some sentences are choppy. There are a few mistakes.

### Try Harder

☐ The beginning is missing or doesn't tell my topic.

☐ Many steps are missing. There are almost no details.

☐ The steps are not in order. The instructions are confusing.

☐ There are no exact words. I can't hear my voice at all.

☐ Most sentences are choppy. Mistakes make it hard to read.

Name _____

# Using Exact Nouns

**Circle the letter of the noun that best replaces each
underlined word or phrase.**

1. Do you want to be a movie person who acts?

   a. lawyer      b. watcher      c. star      d. Venus

2. First, you need to have a good head of fuzzy stuff.

   a. hair      b. ears      c. smile      d. connections

3. Then, you need some cool clothes and a pair of
   dark eye things.

   a. pupils      b. carrots      c. cups      d. sunglasses

4. Next, you need a big, fancy house with a big thing of water.

   a. garage      b. door      c. pool      d. yard

5. You'll need to eat at all the best eating places.

   a. restaurants      b. stations      c. rinks      d. garages

6. Of course, you need to have an agent and a person who
   represents you legally.

   a. judge      b. sheriff      c. lawyer      d. partner

7. Do you need any actual acting stuff?

   a. manners      b. talent      c. rules      d. clothes

8. "It helps, but it's not a must," say all the top Hollywood movie leaders.

   a. sleepers      b. sellers      c. drivers      d. directors

Name _____

# Spelling Words

Look for spelling patterns you have learned to help you remember the Spelling Words on this page. Think about the parts that you find hard to spell.

**Write the missing letters and apostrophe in the Spelling Words below.**

1. n ____ ____

2. o ____ ____

3. f ____ r

4. ____ ____ most

5. ____ ____ so

6. can ____ ____

7. ca ____ ____ ot

8. ab ____ ____ t

9. ____ ____ ways

10. ____ ____ day

11. unt ____ ____

12. ag ____ ____ n

**Study List** On another sheet of paper, write each Spelling Word. Check the list to be sure you spell each word correctly.

112   Theme 2: **Celebrating Traditions**

## Spelling Words

1. now
2. off
3. for
4. almost
5. also
6. can't
7. cannot
8. about
9. always
10. today
11. until
12. again

Name _____

# Spelling Spree

**Word Switch** For each sentence, write a Spelling Word to take the place of the underlined word or words.

Spelling Words

1. Let's go ride the roller coaster <u>another time</u>!
2. I'm in a real hurry, so I can't talk <u>at this time</u>.
3. Sofia <u>every time</u> has a box of raisins in her lunch.
4. My mom said that you can come to the beach <u>too</u>, if you want.
5. It's been <u>not quite</u> three years since we had a snowstorm.
6. They said on the radio that <u>the current day</u> is the first day of fall.

**Spelling Words**

1. now
2. off
3. for
4. almost
5. also
6. can't
7. cannot
8. about
9. always
10. today
11. until
12. again

1. _____   4. _____

2. _____   5. _____

3. _____   6. _____

**Letter Math** Add and subtract letters from the words below to make Spelling Words. Write the new words.

7. foot – ot + r = _____

8. cart – rt + n't = _____

9. able – le + out = _____

10. order – rder + ff = _____

11. canned – ed + ot = _____

12. unit – it + til = _____

Theme 2: **Celebrating Traditions**   113

Name _____

# Proofreading and Writing

**Proofreading** Find and circle the four misspelled Spelling Words in this poster. Then write each word correctly.

### Brazilian Festival

On June 15$^{th}$, the annual Brazilian Festival will take place agin. There will be plenty of traditional music, dancing, and Brazilian food. Our festival is allways a good time. And if you miss this one, you won't get another chance until next year! Tickets are on sale know. Buy yours todday!

**Spelling Words**

1. now
2. off
3. for
4. almost
5. also
6. can't
7. cannot
8. about
9. always
10. today
11. until
12. again

1. _____    3. _____

2. _____    4. _____

**Write a Poem** Think about a tradition that's important to you. It can be one shared by a lot of people, or one that just your family shares. Then write a poem about the tradition. Use Spelling Words from the list.

Name _____

# Musical Words

**Label each sentence True or False. If the sentence is false, rewrite it to make it correct.**

1. A **conga** is played like a trumpet.

_____

_____

2. **Percussion** instruments are played by being struck or shaken.

_____

_____

3. **Performing** is done with no one around.

_____

_____

4. A **record** is shaped like a square.

_____

_____

5. **Salsa** is a style of Latin American dance music.

_____

_____

6. A **theater** is a building where plays, movies, or concerts are presented.

_____

_____

Name _____

# Categories Chart

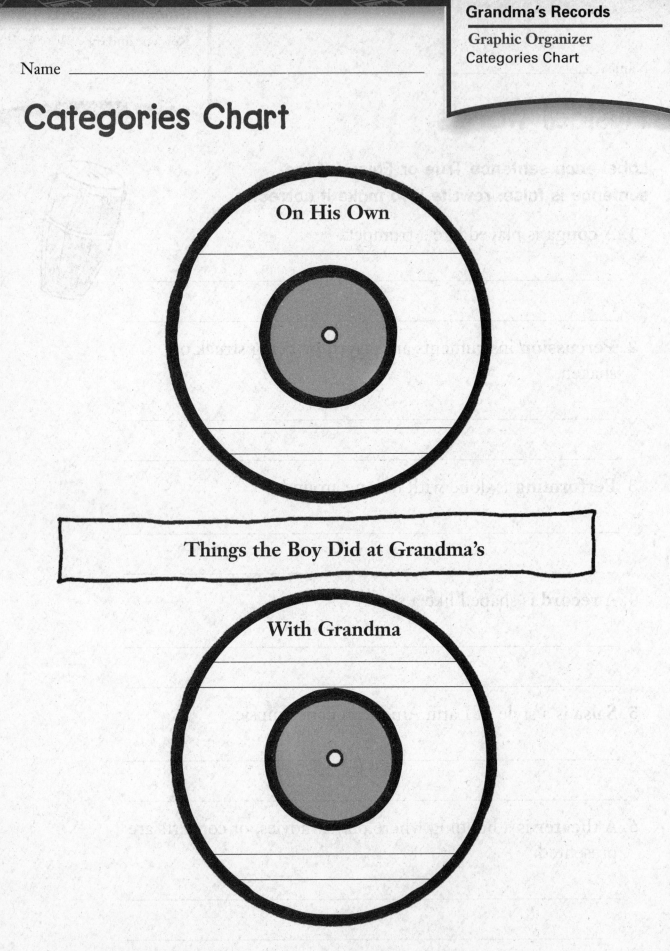

**On His Own**

**Things the Boy Did at Grandma's**

**With Grandma**

Name _____

# Read All About It!

**Answer the reporter's questions as if you were the grown-up narrator. Use complete sentences.**

1. Where did you spend your summers as a boy?

_____

_____

2. What did you and your grandmother do all summer?

_____

_____

3. What else did you like to do?

_____

_____

4. Did you ever go anywhere special with Grandma?

_____

_____

5. What happened at the concert?

_____

_____

6. What do you do now that you're grown up?

_____

Name _____

# Family Categories

**Read the story. Then complete the chart on the next page.**

## No Time to Spare

It's hard to find a good time to get in touch with my Aunt Mickey Sobol. It's even harder to reach my cousins Karen and Ike. That's because they're always busy.

Their day starts at sunup when Karen and Ike head for the barn to feed their sheep. Meanwhile, Aunt Mickey does chores and fixes the lunches. After breakfast, my cousins take the bus to school, and Aunt Mickey leaves for work.

Each day, Aunt Mickey walks a mile to the little store she runs by the lake. People from nearby vacation homes often stop there, so she's always busy.

After school, Karen and Ike head for the animal shelter down the road. Both of them want to be animal doctors, so they like to help with the animals.

After dinner and homework, the family relaxes. Ike usually reads, and Karen talks to a friend on the computer. Aunt Mickey enjoys weaving colorful blankets made of wool from their sheep.

Name _____

# Family Categories

**Write story details to complete this chart.**

**Family Members**
_____
_____
_____

**Places Near Their Home**
their barn
_____
_____
_____

**The Sobol Family**

**Activities**
going to school
_____
_____
_____
_____
_____

Theme 2: **Celebrating Traditions**     119

Name _____

# Perfect Plurals

► Add *-s* to form the plural of most nouns.
hat / hat**s**

► Add *-es* to form the plural of nouns that end in *ch*.
lunch / lunch**es**

► When a noun ends with a consonant and *y*,
change the *y* to *i* and add *-es*.
penn**y** / penn**ies**

**Write the plural of the word that matches each clue in the puzzle. Use the Word Bank for help.**

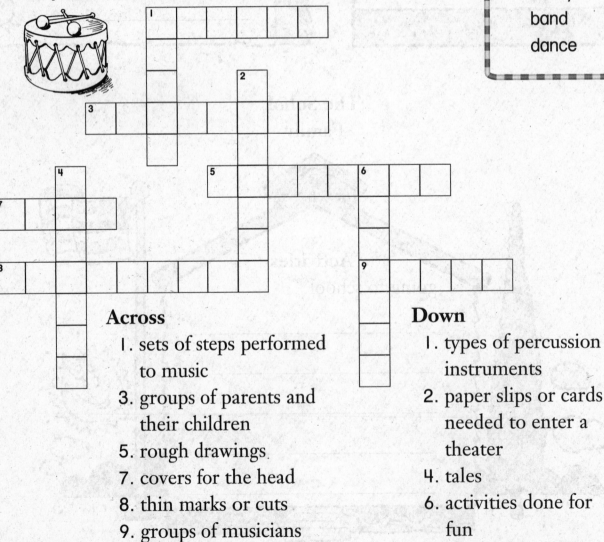

**Across**

1. sets of steps performed to music
3. groups of parents and their children
5. rough drawings
7. covers for the head
8. thin marks or cuts
9. groups of musicians

**Down**

1. types of percussion instruments
2. paper slips or cards needed to enter a theater
4. tales
6. activities done for fun

Name _____

# The Long *o* Sound

To spell a word with the /ō/ sound, remember that this sound can be spelled *oa*, *ow*, or *o*.

/ō/     oa, ow, o     c**oa**ch, bl**ow**, h**o**ld

► In the words *sew* and *though*, the /ō/ sound is spelled *ew* and *ough*.

**Write each Spelling Word under its spelling of the /ō/ sound.**

**Spelling Words**

1. coach
2. blow
3. float
4. hold
5. sew
6. though*
7. sold
8. soap
9. row
10. own
11. both
12. most

### *oa* Spelling

_____

_____

_____

### *o* Spelling

_____

_____

_____

### *ow* Spelling

_____

_____

### **Another Spelling**

_____

Name _____

# Spelling Spree

**Word Maze** Begin at the arrow and follow the Word Maze to find seven Spelling Words. Write the words in order.

eanblowfpthoughrwfloatvhold soldrxwboththeisold

1. _____   5. _____

2. _____   6. _____

3. _____   7. _____

4. _____

**Classifying** Write the Spelling Word that belongs in each group of words.

8. have, possess, _____

9. mend, stitch, _____

10. teacher, trainer, _____

11. toothpaste, shampoo, _____

12. lots, many, _____

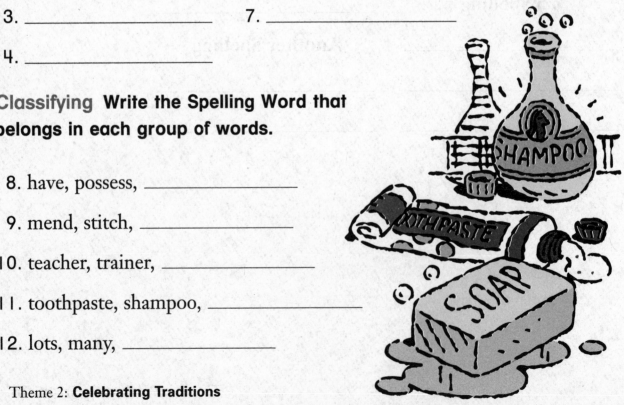

Name _____

# Proofreading and Writing

**Proofreading** Circle the five misspelled Spelling Words in this poster. Then write each word correctly.

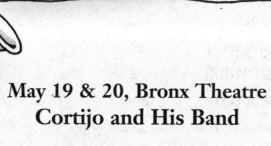

**May 19 & 20, Bronx Theatre
Cortijo and His Band**

See the moast exciting band in Puerto Rico!

You won't believe your oun ears! This music is

the best in New York. Tickets for bothe nights

will be soled at the box office. You will want to

sit in the first rowe!

**Spelling Words**

1. coach
2. blow
3. float
4. hold
5. sew
6. though*
7. sold
8. soap
9. row
10. own
11. both
12. most

1. _____    4. _____

2. _____    5. _____

3. _____

**Write a Story About Yourself** Have you ever shared a special event with a family member or a friend? Maybe it was a concert, a party, or even a trip.

**On a separate sheet of paper, write about a time when you shared a special event with a family member or a friend. Tell what the experience was like. Use Spelling Words from the list.**

Name _____

# Word Sort

**Parts of a Dictionary** Read each word. Then alphabetize
the words and place each word with the correct guide words.

| | | |
|---|---|---|
| snore | lentil | outing |
| outfit | outgoing | lent |
| lesson | snowdrift | outlet |
| snow | leopard | snout |

**lengthy/let**

_____

_____

_____

_____

**snip/snowdrop**

_____

_____

_____

_____

**outfielder/outnumber**

_____

_____

_____

Name _____

# Capital Letters

**Capitalize each proper noun on the list below.**

1. carmen maldonado _____

2. pennsylvania _____

3. tuesday _____

4. fifth avenue _____

5. jon carlson smith _____

6. fourth of july _____

7. united states of america _____

8. *the keeping quilt* _____

9. mary ellen _____

10. mexico city, mexico _____

**Write the proper noun or nouns in each sentence.**

11. After school, Dad took me to the library. _____

12. We will go to the Westfield Fair on Saturday _____

13. Liz wants to visit Colorado. _____

14. My family plans to travel in Canada. _____

15. We will go during the last week of June. _____

Name _____

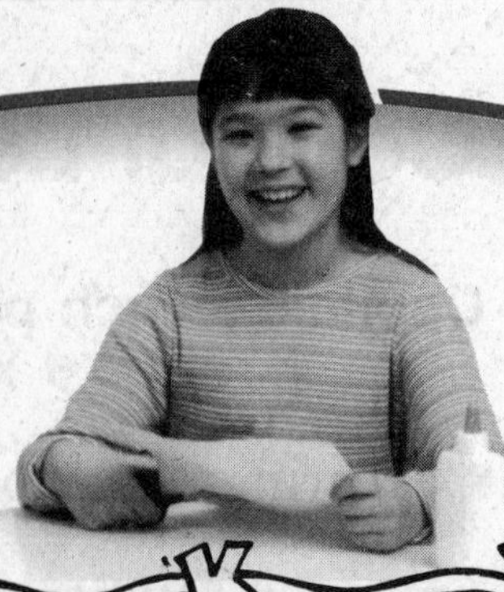

# Charting Capital Letters

**This chart shows common and proper nouns. Add one more proper noun for each common noun in the chart.**

| | Common Noun | Proper Noun |
|---|---|---|
| **people** | author | Eric Velasquez _____ |
| | family member | Grandma _____ |
| **places** | country | Spain _____ |
| | state | Ohio _____ |
| | city | Detroit _____ |
| | street | Elm Street _____ |
| | school | Vale Elementary School _____ |
| | store | Blue Goose Pet Shop _____ |
| **things** | river | Rio Grande _____ |
| | month | September _____ |
| | day | Wednesday _____ |
| | language | Spanish _____ |

Name _____

# Proper Nouns

Remember that titles and their abbreviations, when used with a person's name, begin with a capital letter. Use a capital letter for a person's initials. End abbreviated titles with a period.

**Proofread the letter below. Find the proper nouns and titles that need capital letters. Look for abbreviations that need periods. Use the proofreading marks to show the correction.**

| Proofreading Marks | |
|---|---|
| Make a small letter: | Çity |
| Make a capital letter: | boston |
| Add a period: | Mr⊙ |

Mr Jason Brown
326 winter Drive
Brooklyn, NY 11236

Dear Jason,

   Hello from puerto rico! My family and I are staying in santurce with our friend dr R T vasquez. My grandmother, Carmen, grew up here.

   Later we will visit san juan, which is a big city. On our way back to New york, we will stop in miami, florida.

   I can't wait to show my pictures to you and sam. Our teacher, ms miller, will love the photographs of gardens.

                    See you soon,

                    eric

# A Character Sketch

**Use this page to help you plan a character sketch. Write whom your character sketch will be about. Then write at least two interesting details about what the person looks like, what the person says and does, and how you feel about the person. The details should help you to describe the person.**

**My Character**

_____

_____

### How the Person Looks

1. _____

2. _____

3. _____

### What the Person Does

1. _____

2. _____

3. _____

### What the Person Says

1. _____

_____

2. _____

_____

3. _____

_____

### My Feelings About the Person

1. _____

2. _____

3. _____

**Write your character sketch on a separate sheet of paper. Use the details above.**

# Correcting Run-On Sentences

► Two or more sentences that run together
make a **run-on sentence**.

► Correct run-on sentences by making separate sentences.
Add sentence end marks and capital letters where they are needed.

**Run-On Sentence:**

My friend Patricia loves to dance, she studies ballet every Saturday.

**Corrected Sentences:**

My friend Patricia loves to dance. **S**he studies ballet every Saturday.

**If the sentence is correct, write** *Correct.* **If it is a run-on sentence,
write it as two sentences.**

1. My favorite singer is Gloria Estefan, she sings great songs.

_____

_____

2. My father runs a restaurant in town, he's the best cook in the world.

_____

_____

3. My mother is a math teacher at Yorkstone High School.

_____

_____

4. My sister Tasha loves gymnastics, she does the best cartwheels.

_____

_____

Name _____

# Word Search

**Write the letter of the correct definition next to each word. Then find the words in the puzzle and circle them.**

1. wealth _____

2. royalty _____

3. collection _____

4. embroidered _____

5. symbols _____

6. flourish _____

a. decorated by sewing

b. kings and queens

c. lots of money or belongings

d. drawings that stand for something

e. a group of items with something in common

f. a showy waving motion

| E | M | B | R | O | I | D | E | R | E | D | D | D |
|---|---|---|---|---|---|---|---|---|---|---|---|---|
| K | J | J | M | F | C | O | Q | W | H | R | G | N |
| O | L | U | J | Y | R | R | O | Y | A | L | T | Y |
| R | O | Q | I | P | C | C | O | S | H | T | C | A |
| X | S | L | D | E | E | O | W | V | E | O | J | N |
| F | P | X | C | C | O | L | L | E | C | T | O | R |
| H | L | J | J | M | F | L | O | U | R | I | S | H |
| L | V | I | M | G | C | E | U | U | N | N | J | B |
| N | E | F | W | I | M | C | P | W | W | D | J | S |
| S | S | W | E | A | L | T | H | L | P | Z | K | J |
| S | E | C | J | W | S | I | J | E | L | M | E | L |
| W | Y | S | Y | M | B | O | L | S | U | R | Q | W |
| N | T | R | J | B | V | N | D | Y | Y | S | X | O |

130    Theme 2: **Celebrating Traditions**

Name _____

# Cluster Maps

Aunt
Phoebe

adinkra
cloth

Theme 2: **Celebrating Traditions**    131

Name _____

# What the Cloth Says

**Complete these sentences about *The Talking Cloth*.**

Aunt Phoebe tells Amber about many things.  Today they

talk about _____.  At one

time, only _____ wore it.

Amber learns that the cloth talks because the colors and

symbols _____.  If the cloth is

white, that means _____.  If it is blue,

that means _____.  The symbols on it

stand for ideas like _____ and

_____.

Aunt Phoebe wraps the cloth around Amber.  Now she

feels as if she's an _____ with

_____ gathered

around her.

Name _____

# Details for Playing

**Read the story.  Then complete the chart on the next page.**

## Not for Sale

As Zack walked along, he passed stores with window displays that didn't interest him.  Then he came to a store window full of old, worn things.  A strange object caught his eye.  The wood was dark and shiny smooth. It was long, about as long as Zack's arm, and had six little bowls along each of its sides.  At each end was a larger bowl, which made fourteen little bowls in all.

Curious, Zack went inside for a better look.  Noting Zack's interest, the shopkeeper explained that the wooden object was a game board carved by an Ashanti artist in Ghana, Africa.  The shopkeeper pulled up two chairs and told Zack to sit down.  Then he scooped out some brown seeds from one of the bowls and showed Zack how to play *wari*, an Ashanti board game.

At least once a week Zack stopped by the shop to play *wari* with Mr. Oban, the shopkeeper.  Both he and Mr. Oban enjoyed playing.  And when they finished,  Mr. Oban always put the game board away in the back room.  It was no longer for sale.

Name _____

# Details for Playing

continued

**Complete this chart. List details from
the story "Not for Sale."**

| List of Details |
|---|
| **the game board** |
| 1. _____ |
| 2. _____ |
| 3. _____ |
| 4. _____ |
| **Zack's feelings** |
| 1. _____ |
| 2. _____ |
| **Zack's actions** |
| 1. _____ |
| 2. _____ |
| 3. _____ |
| 4. _____ |

Name _____

# Shorten It!

A **contraction** is the short way of saying or writing two words.
The apostrophe (') takes the place of one or more letters.
**Fill in the spaces below to show how contractions are formed.**

1. he    +   is    =   _____

2. she   +   will   =   _____

3. was   +   not   =   _____

4. they   +   are   =   _____

5. I      +   will   =   _____

6. _____   +   _____   =   it's

7. _____   +   _____   =   you're

8. _____   +   _____   =   hasn't

9. _____   +   _____   =   isn't

10. _____   +   _____   =   we're

# Three-Letter Clusters

When two or more consonants with different sounds are written together, they form a **consonant cluster**. When you are spelling a word that has a consonant cluster, say the word aloud and listen for the different consonant sounds. Remember, some words begin with the consonant clusters *spr*, *str*, and *thr*.

**spr**ing     **str**ong     **thr**ow

Some other words have unexpected spelling patterns.

► A beginning /n/ sound may be spelled *kn*, as in **kn**ee. (The *k* is silent.)

► A beginning /r/ sound may be spelled *wr*, as in **wr**ap. (The *w* is silent.)

► A final /ch/ sound may be spelled *tch*, as in pa**tch**. (The *t* is silent.)

**Write each Spelling Word under its proper category.**

**Spelling Words**

1. spring
2. knee
3. throw
4. patch
5. strong
6. wrap
7. three
8. watch
9. street
10. know
11. spread
12. write

| Three-Letter Clusters | Unexpected Consonant Patterns |
| --- | --- |
| _____ | _____ |
| _____ | _____ |
| _____ | _____ |
| _____ | _____ |
| _____ | _____ |
| _____ | _____ |

Name _____

# Spelling Spree

**Hink Pinks** **Write the Spelling Word that fits the clue
and rhymes with the given word.**

> **Example:** just-born twins   **new** _____ *two*

1. a ball tossed to a baby                    **low** _____
2. jam or jelly                                       **bread** _____
3. cord for a kite on a day in May        _____ **string**
4. you and two friends on a school
   holiday                                            _____ **free**
5. a tidy block to live on                     **neat** _____
6. plastic covering on a bottle top       **cap** _____

1. _____     4. _____

2. _____     5. _____

3. _____     6. _____

**Finding Words** **Write the Spelling Words
in each of these words.**

7. patchwork       _____

8. headstrong      _____

9. kneecap          _____

10. wristwatch     _____

11. knowing         _____

12. writer            _____

**Spelling Words**

1. spring
2. knee
3. throw
4. patch
5. strong
6. wrap
7. three
8. watch
9. street
10. know
11. spread
12. write

# Proofreading and Writing

**Proofreading** Circle the five misspelled Spelling
Words in this character sketch.  Then write each
word correctly on the lines below.

Amber's aunt has been everywhere.  Aunt
Phoebe takes a long trip to a faraway place every
springe.  She has been to Africa thee times.  When
she visits a foreign country, she wants to nowe what it
is like to live there.  Every time she walks down a new
street, she likes to wache the people carefully.  She
notices how they dress and listens to how they speak.
Later, she always takes the time to rite to Amber
about her experiences.  I admire Aunt Phoebe because
she is always learning something new.

1. spring
2. knee
3. throw
4. patch
5. strong
6. wrap
7. three
8. watch
9. street
10. know
11. spread
12. write

1. _____    4. _____

2. _____    5. _____

3. _____

**Write a Thank-You Note** Has a relative or friend ever given
you a special or unusual gift?  What was it that made it special?

**On a separate sheet of paper, write a thank-you note for the
gift.  Make sure to tell the person you are thanking why the gift
is special to you.  Use Spelling Words from the list.**

Name _____

# Rhyming Crossword

**Complete the crossword puzzle by writing the correct rhyme for each word. Remember that a rhyming word has the same end sound as another word. Choose your answers from the words in the box.**

## Vocabulary

trip

maps

lace

cause

wealth

silk

smiles

sled

smells

might

## Across

2. Object used to go across snow.
   Rhymes with *said*.

3. A happy person does this.
   Rhymes with *miles*.

7. A piece of string used to tie a shoe.
   Rhymes with *face*.

8. Riches. Rhymes with *health*.

9. A voyage. Rhymes with *lip*.

10. Drawings of the earth's surface.
    Rhymes with *traps*.

## Down

1. What your nose does.
   Rhymes with *tells*.

4. Strength. Rhymes with *right*.

5. A smooth, shiny fabric.
   Rhymes with *milk*.

6. A reason.
   Rhymes with *pause*.

Name _____

# Circling Nouns

**Circle each singular common noun in the sentences below.
Underline each plural common noun.**

1. Aunt Phoebe collects many things.

2. The cloth is embroidered in sections.

3. The fabric has no patches.

4. The patterns show many colors and shapes.

5. Phoebe gave her niece two boxes.

6. Inside, she found two colorful dresses.

**Write each plural noun in the correct column below.**

**Add -*s* to form the plural**          **Add -*es* to form the plural**

_____          _____

_____          _____

_____          _____

_____

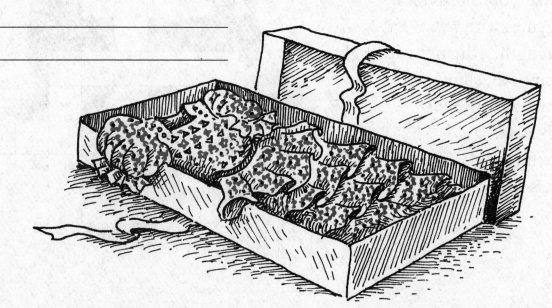

Name _____

# Puzzling Plurals

Complete the puzzle by writing the plural of each noun.
Each noun is used only once.  Some letters are filled in
to help you get started.

**Across**

princess _____

basket _____

number _____

thing _____

tale _____

**Down**

symbol _____

box _____

word _____

pattern _____

dress _____

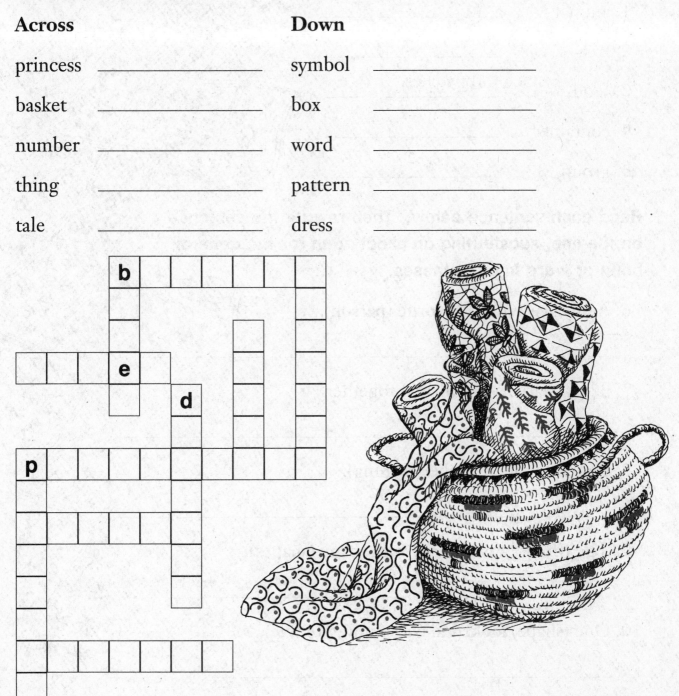

Name _____

# Using Exact Nouns

**Write a noun that is more exact than each general noun below.**

1. animal _____

2. tree _____

3. food _____

4. container _____

5. group _____

**Read each sentence below. Then rewrite the sentence on the line, substituting an exact noun for the general noun or word in parentheses.**

6. Amber visited her favorite (person).

_____

7. They shared a hot (drink) together.

_____

8. Phoebe showed Amber a (thing).

_____

9. The (thing) was covered with many (shapes).

_____

10. One (shape) looked like a spinning (circle).

_____

# Writing an Answer to a Question

When you write an answer to a
question, follow these guidelines.

► Read the question carefully.

► Look for key words to help you decide
what information the question is asking for.

► Give facts and examples that provide the information asked for.

**For each question, write your answer on the lines. Write the start of
the answer on the first answer line. Write the rest of the answer on the
other answer lines.**

1. **Question:** What holiday do you enjoy most? Explain why.
   **Turn the question into a statement.**

   _____

   **Give facts that answer the question.**

   _____

   _____

2. **Question:** What place would you like to visit most? Explain why.
   **Turn the question into a statement.**

   _____

   **Give facts that answer the question.**

   _____

   _____

Name _____

# Writing Complete Sentences

A complete sentence contains both a naming part
and an action part.

| **Naming Part** | **Action Part** |
|---|---|
| Aunt Phoebe | bought the adinkra cloth in Africa. |

A sentence fragment is an incomplete sentence that has
just one sentence part.

**Fragment (naming part only)** The Ashanti people.
**Fragment (action part only)** Made adinkra cloths.

A complete sentence begins with a capital letter and ends
with the correct end punctuation.z

**Read each item. Write** Complete Sentence **if the sentence
has both a naming part and an action part. If the item is a
sentence fragment, make it a complete sentence by adding
words. Write your complete sentence correctly.**

1. Means gold or riches. _____

_____

2. Amber and her father. _____

_____

3. Aunt Phoebe tells stories to Amber. _____

_____

4. Drinks hot mocha. _____

_____

Name _____

# What Do You Think?

**Answer the questions below. Use your glossary if you need help.**

1. Who are some of your ancestors? Where did they live?

   _____

   _____

2. What could someone do to honor his or her parents or family members?

   _____

   _____

3. What is something you have learned by imitating another person?

   _____

   _____

4. What can you do to show respect for your teacher?

   _____

   _____

5. How should young people act toward their elders?

   _____

   _____

Name _____

# Cluster Diagram

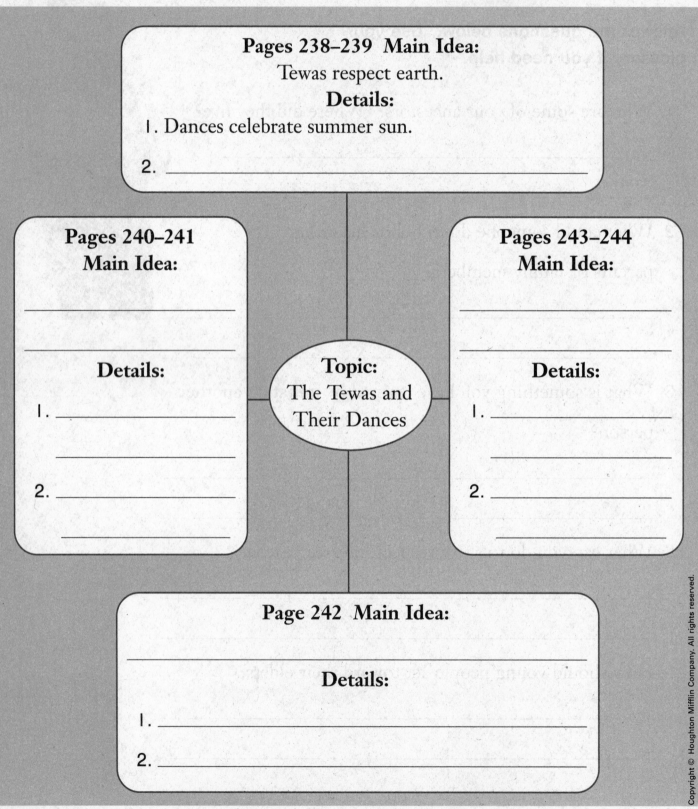

**Pages 238–239  Main Idea:**

Tewas respect earth.

**Details:**

1. Dances celebrate summer sun.

2. _____

**Pages 240–241
Main Idea:**

_____

_____

**Details:**

1. _____

_____

2. _____

_____

**Topic:**
The Tewas and
Their Dances

**Pages 243–244
Main Idea:**

_____

_____

**Details:**

1. _____

_____

2. _____

_____

**Page 242  Main Idea:**

_____

**Details:**

1. _____

2. _____

Name _____

# Feast Day Questions

**Answer each question about *Dancing Rainbows*.
Use complete sentences.**

1. What is Feast Day?

   _____

   _____

   _____

2. Why do Curt, Andy, and the other Tewa people dance on Feast Day?

   _____

   _____

3. What sounds might you hear on Feast Day in the plaza?

   _____

   _____

4. When the Tewas dance, what might you see?

   _____

   _____

   _____

5. What did Andy do for his grandson and other young Tewas?

   _____

   _____

Name _____

# Mainly Ideas

**Read the article. Then complete the diagram on the next page.**

## All About Eagles

How many different kinds of eagles do you think live in the world? If you guessed about sixty, you'd be right. Some kinds of eagles are large and some are small. Most are strong for their size. Some are even strong enough to lift food weighing almost as much as they do!

Eagles have been used as symbols of power and freedom. Some people call them the "king of birds" because of their strength and brave, proud looks. In 1782, the United States of America chose the bald eagle as its national bird.

Bald eagles are among the larger eagles. They can weigh anywhere from eight to thirteen pounds. These great birds can have wings that spread as much as seven feet across! Their heads are covered with white feathers, making them look "bald" from a distance.

Name _____

# Mainly Ideas continued

## Complete the diagram with facts from "All About Eagles."

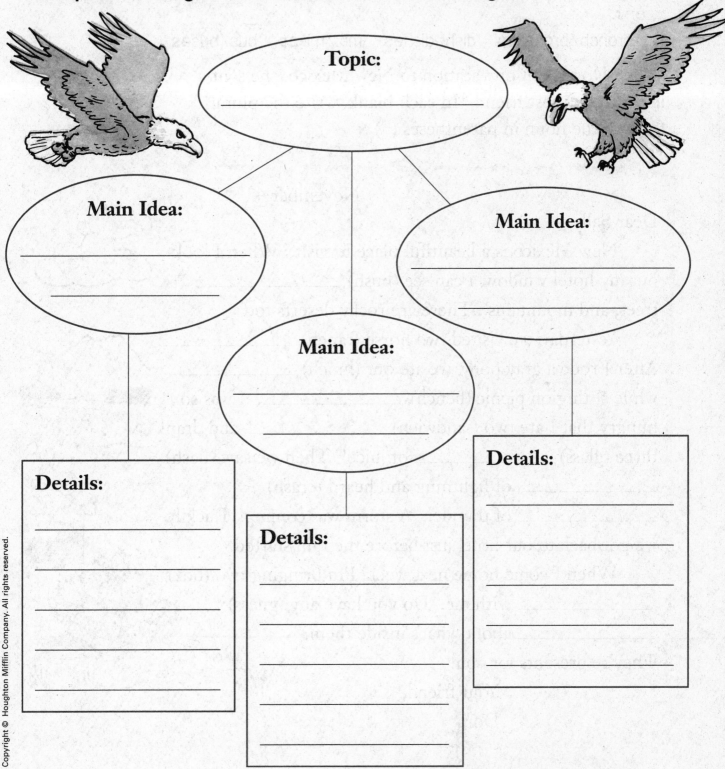

Topic:
_____

Main Idea:
_____
_____

Main Idea:
_____
_____

Main Idea:
_____
_____

Details:
_____
_____
_____
_____

Details:
_____
_____
_____
_____

Details:
_____
_____
_____
_____

**Dancing Rainbows**

Structural Analysis
Plurals of Words Ending in
*ch, sh, x, s*

Name _____

# More and More Plurals

Add *-es* to form the plural of a singular noun that ends in *ch, sh, x,* or *s*.

branch/branch**es**   dish/dish**es**   mix/mix**es**   bus/bus**es**

When Dora went on vacation to New Mexico, she sent a letter to her best friend. In each blank, write the plural form of the noun in parentheses ( ).

> November 4
>
> Dear Sally,
>
> New Mexico is a beautiful place to visit. When I look out my hotel window, I can see (bush) _____, trees, and mountains. There are rocky deserts too.
>
> Yesterday, we visited two horse (ranch) _____. After I rode a gray pony, we ate our (lunch) _____ while sitting on picnic (bench) _____. I was so hungry that I ate two (sandwich) _____ and drank three (glass) _____ of juice! Then we saw (flash) _____ of lightning and heard (crash) _____ of thunder. A storm was coming! Luckily, we got back to our hotel just before the rain started.
>
> When I come home next week, I'm bringing two (box) _____ with me. Do you have any (guess) _____ about what's inside them? They're presents for you!
>
> Your friend,
> Dora

Name _____

# The Long *i* Sound

When you hear the /ī/ sound, think of the patterns *igh*, *i*, and *ie*.

/ī/ br**igh**t, w**i**ld, d**ie**

**Write each Spelling Word under its spelling of the /ī/ sound.**

1. wild
2. bright
3. die
4. sight
5. child
6. pie
7. fight
8. lie
9. tight
10. tie
11. might
12. mind

*igh* **Spelling**

_____
_____
_____
_____

*ie* **Spelling**

_____
_____

*i* **Spelling**

_____
_____

Name _____

# Spelling Spree

**Sentence Pairs** Write the Spelling Word that best
completes each pair of sentences.

**Example:** A jet does not fly low. It flies <u>*high*</u>.

**Spelling Words**

1. wild
2. bright
3. die
4. sight
5. child
6. pie
7. fight
8. lie
9. tight
10. tie
11. might
12. mind

1. These shoes are not loose.  They are _____.
2. My sister is not a grownup.  She is a _____.
3. A tiger is not tame.  It is _____.
4. I will not have cake for dessert.  I will have _____.
5. Neither team won.  The score was a _____.
6. The sunshine is not dim today.  It is _____.
7. He did not tell the truth.  He told a_____.

1. _____     5. _____

2. _____     6. _____

3. _____     7. _____

4. _____

**Missing Letters** Each missing letter fits in ABC
order between the other two letters.  Write the
missing letters to spell a Spelling Word.

**Example:** e _ g  h _ j  m _ o  c _ e  *find*

8. c _ e  h _ j  d _ f         8. _____

9. l _ n  h _ j  m _ o  c _ e    9. _____

10. e _ g  h _ j  f _ h  g _ i  s _ u   10. _____

Name _____

# Proofreading and Writing

**Proofreading** Circle the five misspelled Spelling Words in this page from a travel brochure. Then write each word correctly.

**Visit Beautiful New Mexico!**

Come to New Mexico and discover a land of amazing beauty! Explore wonderful deserts bathed in brit sunshine. Hike in our mountains and experience adventure in the wilde! Relax your minde and body at one of our many resorts. Enjoy the siet of colorful hot-air balloons in Albuquerque. Spend a week with us, and you just mieght never go home again! That's no lie.

**Spelling Words**

1. wild
2. bright
3. die
4. sight
5. child
6. pie
7. fight
8. lie
9. tight
10. tie
11. might
12. mind

1. _____  3. _____  5. _____

2. _____  4. _____

**Write an Explanation** The Tewas believe that the eagle is a special animal that carries messages to earth. If you could wear an animal costume, what animal would you choose to be?

**On a separate sheet of paper, tell what animal you would choose and explain why you think this animal is special. Use Spelling Words from the list.**

Name _____

# Definition Derby

**Read the dictionary entry for the word *dance*. Then write sample sentences as directed.**

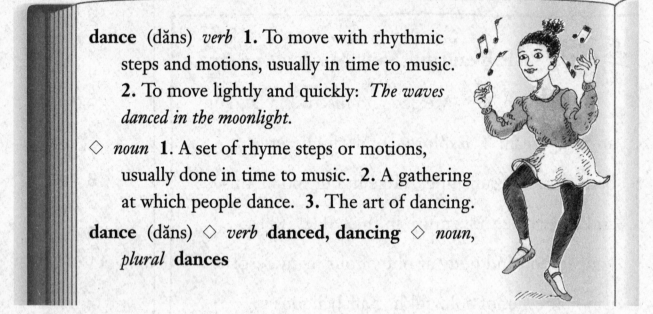

**dance** (dăns) *verb* **1.** To move with rhythmic steps and motions, usually in time to music. **2.** To move lightly and quickly: *The waves danced in the moonlight.*

◇ *noun* **1.** A set of rhyme steps or motions, usually done in time to music. **2.** A gathering at which people dance. **3.** The art of dancing.

**dance** (dăns) ◇ *verb* **danced, dancing** ◇ *noun, plural* **dances**

1. Write a sentence using the most common meaning of *dance*.

_____

2. Write a sentence using noun definition number 3.

_____

3. Write a sentence using noun definition number 1.

_____

4. Write a sentence using verb definition number 2.

_____

5. Write a sentence using the least common meaning of *dance*.

_____

Name _____

# Beat the Drum for Plurals

**Circle all the plural nouns and write each one in the correctly labeled drum.**

1. The Tewa children practice dancing.
2. Men and women prepare for a festival.
3. The skies are clear and blue.
4. Families arrive from many different cities.
5. The parties are about to begin.
6. Loaves of bread are stacked on the table.
7. People stomp their feet.
8. Sweet candies are a special treat.

**Change _y_ to _i_ and add -_es_**

_____

_____

_____

_____

_____

**Special Plural Forms**

_____

_____

_____

_____

_____

_____

Name _____

# Completing with Plurals

**Complete the story by writing the plural form for each noun in parentheses.**

1. The _____ are sunny and clear. (sky)

2. All the relatives help bake many _____ of

   bread for the feast. (loaf)

3. Many _____ have come to the celebration.

   (family)

4. At last, six _____ begin to dance. (man)

5. Their _____ fly above the ground. (foot)

Name _____

# Proofreading for Noun Endings

**Proofread the paragraphs below. Find plurals of nouns that are spelled incorrectly. Circle each misspelled plural. Then write each correctly spelled noun on the lines below. Use a dictionary for help.**

After sunrise, the Tewa mens and womens gather.
Mothers carry their smiling babys. Fatheres walk with
their sons and daughters. People arrive from many citys.
They look forward to the dances and the storys.

Three childs wear buffalo costumies. They are
dancers. Their feet move in beautiful patterns. After the
dance, everyone feasts on loafs of bread and tasty treats.

| Regular | Ends in consonant + *y* | Special plurals |
|---------|------------------------|-----------------|
| _____ | _____ | _____ |
| _____ | _____ | _____ |
| _____ | _____ | _____ |

Name _____

# Writing a News Article

**Use this page to plan and organize your news article about a holiday or celebration. When you finish, use the outline to write your article on a separate sheet of paper.**

1. Holiday or Celebration _____

_____

2. Who? _____

_____

3. What? _____

_____

4. When? _____

_____

5. Where? _____

_____

6. Why? _____

_____

7. How? _____

_____

8. Interesting Opening Sentence _____

_____

9. Interesting Headline _____

Name _____

# Newspaper Article

**Audience** A good newspaper article includes details that help
the audience picture what they did not witness themselves.

**Read the newspaper article. Then answer each question
based on some facts or details from the article.**

> In the past month, San Juan Pueblo has had no rain. The
> elders of the Tewa tribe who live there have decided to hold a
> rain dance. The dancing will begin at nine in the morning and
> last until noon. The purpose of the dance is to ask the Tewa
> ancestors to bring rain. Andy Garcia is an elder of the tribe.
> He says that the Tewa believe that their ancestors come back as
> raindrops to water their crops and give them water to drink.

1. Who are the Tewa?

_____

2. Where will the rain dance be held?

_____

3. What would make an interesting beginning to the article?

_____

_____

_____

4. What would make an interesting headline for this article?

_____

**Congratulations! You are a good reporter! Now write your new,
improved article on a separate piece of paper.**

Name _____

# A Blossoming Crossword

**In the crossword, write the vocabulary word that matches each clue. Write one letter in each box.**

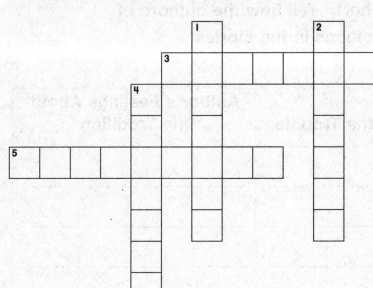

## Across

3. large amounts of something
5. high lands near the water

## Down

1. blue and purple flowers
2. what the flowers did when they opened
4. little valleys

Name _____

# Celebrating Chinese New Year

Use story details to finish the chart. Tell how the authors of these stories feel about the traditions in the stories.

| Story | Details About the Tradition | Author's Feelings About the Tradition |
|---|---|---|
| *Miss Rumphius* Tradition: making the world more beautiful | 1. _____ <br> _____ <br> _____ <br> 2. _____ <br> _____ <br> 3. _____ <br> _____ | _____ <br> _____ <br> _____ <br> _____ <br> _____ <br> _____ <br> _____ |
| *Celebrating Chinese New Year* Tradition: Chinese New Year | 1. _____ <br> _____ <br> 2. _____ <br> _____ <br> 3. _____ <br> _____ | _____ <br> _____ <br> _____ <br> _____ <br> _____ <br> _____ |

Name _____

# Traditions Diagram

Fill in the Venn diagram below with details about the traditions in *Miss Rumphius* and *The Keeping Quilt*.

**Miss Rumphius**

Tradition:

_____

Created by:

_____

How Miss Rumphius does it:

_____

Places she does it:

1. _____

2. _____

Passed on to:

_____

**Both Traditions:**

_____

_____

_____

**The Family in
*The Keeping Quilt***

Tradition:

_____

Created by:

_____

Used for:

1. _____

2. _____

Passed on to:

_____

Name _____

# Words for a Feast

**Key Words  Read each sentence.  Then circle the letter of the word or phrase that has almost the same meaning as the underlined word.**

1. The queen decided to bring everyone in the kingdom together.  She wanted to celebrate her country's <u>unity</u>.
   A. togetherness     B. beauty          C. happiness

2. The king and queen would be the <u>hosts</u> of the biggest party in history.
   A. people who visit other people
   B. people who go to fancy hotels
   C. people who invite other people over

3. The <u>chef</u> had never cooked for so many people before.
   A. leader          B. cook          C. firefighter

4. To feed the whole kingdom, he would have to make a great <u>feast</u>.
   A. fancy meal
   B. cooking pot
   C. breakfast cereal

5. He cooked cakes with seven layers and other <u>elaborate</u> dishes.
   A. boring
   B. fancy
   C. easy

Name _____

# Test Practice

**Use the three steps you've learned to complete these sentences about *Celebrating Chinese New Year*. Fill in the circle next to the best answer.**

1. Chinese New Year begins with a _____.

   ○ visit with relatives      ○ big dinner

   ○ parade      ○ trip to the grocery

2. The main idea of *Celebrating Chinese New Year* is that the holiday is a time when _____.

   ○ families get together

   ○ Ryan helps his dad prepare a special meal

   ○ people do not work

   ○ people eat too much food

3. Ryan's father probably cooks _____.

   ○ only duck and chicken

   ○ hamburgers and hot dogs

   ○ tasty holiday meals

   ○ mostly cakes and pies

4. **Connecting/Comparing** The quilt in *The Keeping Quilt* is like the duck and chicken dish prepared by Ryan's father because both remind people of _____.

   ○ happiness      ○ family unity

   ○ national pride      ○ a new year

*Continue on page 166.*

Theme 2: **Celebrating Traditions**    165

# Test Practice continued

5. The author of Celebrating *Chinese New Year* wrote this article to _____.

    ○ explain how to cook a duck

    ○ tell about a special Chinese tradition

    ○ describe Ryan's family

    ○ persuade readers to visit relatives more often

6. If Ryan did not visit his aunt during the first three days of the Chinese New Year, she might _____.

    ○ send him a special gift        ○ prepare him a meal

    ○ invite him to go on a trip      ○ be angry with him

7. Ryan's family shops early for the New Year's Day meal because _____.

    ○ it is bad luck to shop on New Year's Day

    ○ Ryan's father works at a restaurant on New Year's Day

    ○ grocery stores sometimes run out of duck and chicken

    ○ the New Year's Day feast takes many days to prepare

8. **Connecting/Comparing** Think about Ryan in *Celebrating Chinese New Year* and Curt in *Dancing Rainbows*. When they grow up, they will probably both _____.

    ○ go to a parade to celebrate New Year's Day

    ○ teach their children their families' traditions

    ○ learn how to perform the buffalo dance

    ○ go to San Francisco for a holiday celebration

Name _____

# A Community of Categories

**Read the list of things found in the community where Miss Rumphius lives. Write each item in the correct box.**

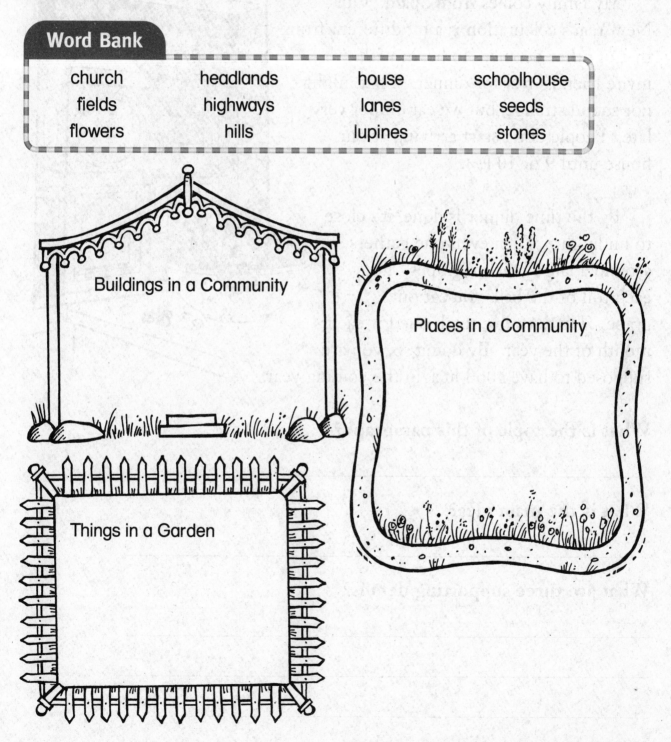

### Word Bank

| | | | |
|---|---|---|---|
| church | headlands | house | schoolhouse |
| fields | highways | lanes | seeds |
| flowers | hills | lupines | stones |

Buildings in a Community

Places in a Community

Things in a Garden

Name _____

# What's It All About?

**Read the paragraphs. Then answer the questions.**

My family comes from Spain. Our New Year's celebration is a bit different from that of other people. To begin with, we invite friends over for dinner. That might not sound strange, but we eat dinner very late. People don't start arriving at our house until 9 or 10 P.M.

By the time dinner is done, it's close to midnight. Then everyone gathers around a large bowl of grapes. For each toll of the bell, you eat one grape. That's twelve total, one for each month of the year. By doing so, you are supposed to have good luck in the coming year.

**What is the topic of this paragraph?**

_____

**What is the main idea?**

_____

**What are three supporting details?**

_____

_____

_____

Name _____

# Contraction Math

**Write the two words that each contraction stands for as an equation. See the example below.**

you're = you + are

1. he'll = _____

2. isn't = _____

3. she's = _____

4. they'll = _____

5. shouldn't = _____

6. we're = _____

7. you'll = _____

8. don't = _____

9. they're = _____

10. you're = _____

Name _____

# Rhyme It!

**To complete the poem below, choose a word from the box that rhymes with each underlined word, and write it on the line.**

We all went walking one by <u>one</u>,
And then we stopped to have some _____.

We all went walking two by <u>two</u>,
And then we stopped to eat some _____.

We all went walking three by <u>three</u>,
And then we stopped to climb a _____.

We all went walking four by <u>four</u>,
And then we stopped at the candy _____.

We all went walking five by <u>five</u>,
And then we stopped to scuba _____.

We all went walking six by <u>six</u>,
And then we stopped to play some _____.

We all went walking seven by <u>seven</u>,
And then we stopped to count to _____.

We all went walking eight by <u>eight</u>,
And then we stopped to roller _____.

We all went walking nine by <u>nine</u>,
And then we stopped to read a _____.

We all went walking ten by <u>ten</u>,
And then we said, "Let's start _____!"

### Word Bank

skate

stew

again

fun

tricks

eleven

tree

sign

dive

store

Name _____

# Spelling Review

**Write Spelling Words from the list to answer the questions.**

1–9. Which nine words have the long *a* or long *e* sound?

1. _____    6. _____

2. _____    7. _____

3. _____    8. _____

4. _____    9. _____

5. _____

10–16. Which seven words have the long *o* sound?

10. _____    14. _____

11. _____    15. _____

12. _____    16. _____

13. _____

17–22. Which six words have the long *i* sound?

17. _____    20. _____

18. _____    21. _____

19. _____    22. _____

23–25. Which three words end with these letters?

23. _____tch        24. _____ead        25. _____ap

23. _____    25. _____

24. _____

## Spelling Words

1. lay
2. feel
3. hold
4. wild
5. might
6. paint
7. seem
8. patch
9. three
10. own
11. speak
12. need
13. lie
14. most
15. spread
16. float
17. row
18. leave
19. both
20. wrap
21. know
22. mind
23. street
24. bright
25. tie

Name _____

# Spelling Spree

**Rhyme Time** Write the Spelling Word that rhymes with the word in dark print.

**Example:** A plump kitty is a ___*fat*___ **cat.**

1. A nice brain is a **kind** _____.

2. An animal life jacket is a **goat** _____.

3. An unreal piece of clothing is a _____ **lie.**

4. Baby triplets are a **wee** _____.

**Word Search** Underline the eight hidden Spelling Words. Then write the words.

**Example:** abeneedlean ___*needle*___

5. redawildell            9. teriloneedum

6. ymightaledfl           10. grpatchibror

7. enrstreetalp           11. olgeraspread

8. knpaintilke            12. wrilleavekn

5. _____    9. _____

6. _____    10. _____

7. _____    11. _____

8. _____    12. _____

**Spelling Words**

1. paint
2. leave
3. might
4. need
5. mind
6. tie
7. spread
8. float
9. three
10. wild
11. patch
12. street

Name _____

# Proofreading and Writing

**Proofreading** Circle the six misspelled Spelling Words in this play. Then write each word correctly.

**Grandpa:** Let's rapp the gifts in brite yellow paper.

**Joe:** We can laye it on the table for Mom.

**Grandpa:** Be careful how you hoald it.

**Joe:** You kno we bouth did a good job!

1. _____   3. _____   5. _____

2. _____   4. _____   6. _____

**Complete a Letter** Use Spelling Words to complete the following letter.

**Spelling Words**

1. lay
2. most
3. wrap
4. lie
5. feel
6. seem
7. hold
8. speak
9. own
10. bright
11. row
12. both
13. know
14. mind

Thanksgiving makes me 7. _____ very happy. Our family has its 8. _____ traditions. My grandfather will 9. _____ his 10. _____ about sharing with others. A feast will 11. _____ on the table, with many plates in a 12. _____. The 13. _____ simple dishes 14. _____ even tastier then.

**Write a Description** On a separate sheet of paper, describe a celebration you enjoy. Use the Spelling Words.

Name _____

# Finding Common Nouns

**Find the common nouns in the announcement.  Write each common noun in the correct garden bed below.**

The students at our school will plant a garden.  We will use the area behind the gym.  All boys and girls can help!  A parent will bring seeds and tools.  You can plant flowers or vegetables.

Name _____

# Finding Proper Nouns

**Read the sentences. Circle each proper noun.**

1. Chinese New Year is a special holiday.

2. This holiday often comes in February.

3. Ryan celebrates this holiday with his family.

4. They invite all their relatives who live
   in San Francisco.

5. Do they buy special foods from the stores on
   Stockton Street?

**This chart lists five common nouns. Add one proper noun for each common noun in the chart.**

|  | Common Noun | Proper Noun |
|---|---|---|
| **people** | friend | _____ |
|  | teacher | _____ |
| **places** | street | _____ |
|  | school | _____ |
| **things** | holiday | _____ |

Name _____

# Tricky Web of Words

**Write the word that matches each clue in the puzzle.**

1. a character who loves to play pranks on others
2. showing off
3. smart
4. traditional story
5. features that make a person special
6. selfish desire for more and more and more
7. bad behavior

## Vocabulary

boastfulness
clever
folktale
greediness
mischief
qualities
trickster

1. __ __ __ (○) __ __ __ __ __
2. __ __ __ __ (○) __ __ __ __ __ __ __
3. (○) __ __ __ __ __ __
4. __ __ __ (○) __ __ __ __
5. (○) __ __ __ __ __ __ __ __
6. (○) __ __ __ __ __ __ __ __ __
7. __ __ __ __ (○) __ __

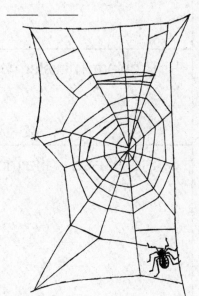

**Read the letters in circles to answer the question.**

What do you call the customs, beliefs, laws, and ways of living that belong to a people?

8. ○○○○○○○

Name _____

# Trickster Story Map

| Story: "Hungry Spider" | Story: "Rabbit Races with Turtle" |
|---|---|
| 1. Trickster | 1. Trickster |
| 2. Trickster's character traits | 2. Trickster's character traits |
| 3. Setting | 3. Setting |
| 4. Problem Trickster needs to solve | 4. Problem Trickster needs to solve |
| 5. Steps used in the trick | 5. Steps used in the trick |
| 6. Results | 6. Results |

Name _____

# It's Tricky

**Compare the three trickster tales.**

▶ Draw a cover cartoon for each tale.
▶ Write enough about the story to make
someone want to read it.

**For example:**
Rabbit races Turtle.
But in the end, Turtle wins!
How does slow Turtle beat
fast Rabbit?

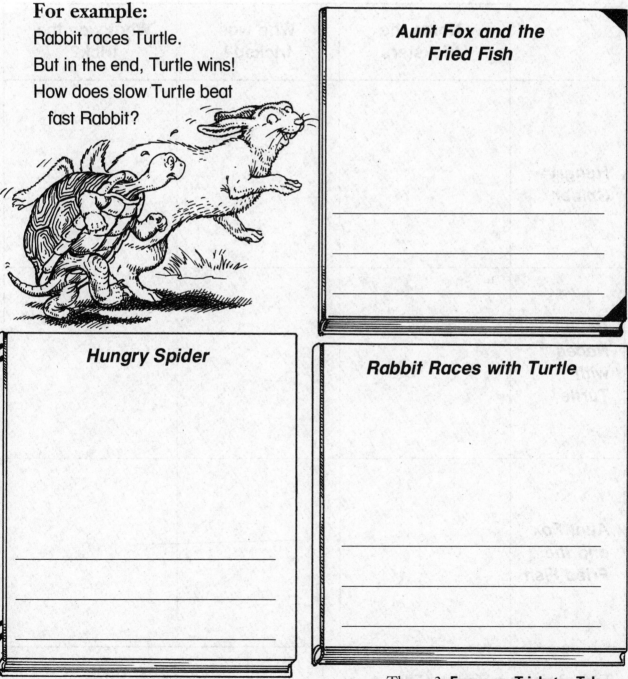

**Aunt Fox and the
Fried Fish**

_____

_____

_____

**Hungry Spider**

_____

_____

**Rabbit Races with Turtle**

_____

_____

_____

Name _____

# What Makes a Trickster Tale?

After reading each selection, complete the chart below to tell why each story is a trickster tale.

| | Name the tricksters | Who was tricked? | What was the trick? |
|---|---|---|---|
| *Hungry Spider* | | | |
| *Rabbit Races with Turtle* | | | |
| *Aunt Fox and the Fried Fish* | | | |

# The Plot of *Aunt Fox* and the Fried Fish

**Fill in the chart, using information from the trickster tale *Aunt Fox and the Fried Fish*.**

**Problem**

_____

_____

**Trick**

Step 1

_____

Step 2

_____

Step 3

_____

Step 4

_____

**Result**

_____

_____

Name _____

# Run, Rabbit, Run

Some base words take *–ed* or *–ing* endings.

| | | |
|---|---|---|
| walk | walk**ed** | walk**ing** |
| jump | jump**ed** | jump**ing** |

When a base word ends in *e*, the *e* is dropped before *–ed* or *–ing*
is added.

| | | |
|---|---|---|
| race | rac**ed** | rac**ing** |
| believe | believ**ed** | believ**ing** |

**Read Rabbit's description of his race.  Circle each word
with an *–ed* or *–ing* ending.  Then write the base words in
the box.**

I was going as fast as I could.  But every
time I turned a corner, Turtle was ahead of
me.  "This is driving me crazy!"  I shouted.
"I know I am faster than a turtle."

    I started zooming even faster.  My feet
hardly touched the ground.  As I crossed the
finish line, I closed my eyes.  I was sure I was
the winner.  I was awfully surprised when I
opened my eyes.  Turtle was already there!

| **Base Words** |
|---|
| 1. _____ |
| 2. _____ |
| 3. _____ |
| 4. _____ |
| 5. _____ |
| 6. _____ |
| 7. _____ |
| 8. _____ |
| 9. _____ |
| 10. _____ |

Name _____

# The Vowel Sound in *join*

The /oi/ sound is spelled with the pattern *oi* or *oy*.

j**oi**n          j**oy**

**Write each Spelling Word under its spelling of the /oi/ sound.**

### *oi* Spelling

_____     _____

_____     _____

_____     _____

_____     _____

_____     _____

### *oy* Spelling

_____

**Spelling Words**

1. join
2. joy
3. boil
4. noise
5. spoil
6. choice
7. soil
8. point
9. foil
10. voice
11. coil
12. broil

Name _____

# Spelling Spree

**Use the Clue** Write the Spelling Word that fits each
clue.

1. You use this to speak.
2. You can wrap food in this.
3. You might find a worm in this.
4. A pencil should have this.
5. Water does this.
6. You might hear this in a big city.

1. _____    4. _____

2. _____    5. _____

3. _____    6. _____

**Letter Math** Write Spelling Words by adding and
taking away letters in the words below.

7. sp + oil = _____    10. voice – v + ch = _____

8. boy – b + j = _____    11. coin – n + l = _____

9. boil + r = _____    12. point – p + j – t = _____

Name _____

# Proofreading and Writing

**Proofreading** Circle the five misspelled Spelling
Words in this short trickster tale. Then write each
word correctly.

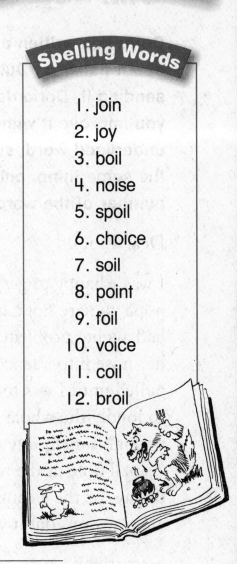

**Spelling Words**

1. join
2. joy
3. boil
4. noise
5. spoil
6. choice
7. soil
8. point
9. foil
10. voice
11. coil
12. broil

### Wolf and Rabbit

Wolf was hungry. She put a pot of water on to
boil, but she had nothing to cook. Then she heard a
nosie — Rabbit was walking by her house!

"Come in and joyn me!" Wolf said in her
sweetest voise. "It would be a joi to have
you for dinner."

"I hate to spoyl your plans," said Rabbit as he
leaped away, "but I think I'll let you eat alone."

1. _____     4. _____

2. _____     5. _____

3. _____

✏️ **Write Instructions** Being a trickster takes planning. Have
you played a trick on a friend or seen someone else play a trick?
What had to be done ahead of time to prepare for the trick?

**On a separate piece of paper, write a set of instructions
that a trickster could use to play a trick. Use Spelling
Words from the list.**

Name _____

# One Degree More

**Daria has written a letter to her friend Eva, telling her all about her trip. But when she rereads the letter before sending it, Daria decides it is not interesting enough. Can you improve it with some strong synonyms? For each underlined word, substitute a word from the box that means the same thing, only more so. Write the synonym after the number of the word it matches**

Dear Eva,

I was 1. <u>happy</u> to get your letter last month. I miss you! I hope you are not 2. <u>upset</u> with me for not writing sooner. I had a 3. <u>big</u> problem to deal with. My puppy, Mitzy, wedged her nose into a fence. I could not get her out! I pulled and pulled until I was too 4. <u>tired</u> to try anymore. Mitzy 5. <u>cried</u> so loudly the whole neighborhood came out to see what was wrong. Finally, my 6. <u>nice</u> neighbor, Ms. Gladly, cut a 7. <u>small</u> hole in the fence so we could pry Mitzy out. I had to pay for the 8. <u>damage</u> Mitzy caused. I guess it all sounds 9. <u>funny</u> now, but it was 10. <u>scary</u> at the time!

| gigantic |
| furious |
| tiny |
| hilarious |
| exhausted |
| wonderful |
| delighted |
| destruction |
| terrifying |
| howled |

Your friend,
Daria

1. _____    6. _____

2. _____    7. _____

3. _____    8. _____

4. _____    9. _____

5. _____    10. _____

Name _____

# Fixing Stringy Sentences

**Correct each stringy sentence by making three simple sentences. Add periods and capital letters where they are needed.**

1. This morning Uncle Fox caught three fish and the fish were big and beautiful and I fried them in the kitchen.

   _____

   _____

2. I also cooked carrots, peas, and potatoes and there was a lot of food and so we decided to ask Uncle Tiger for lunch.

   _____

   _____

**Correct each stringy sentence by making one simple sentence and one compound sentence. Add punctuation and capital letters where they are needed.**

3. I ate all the fish myself and Uncle Tiger arrived and there was nothing to feed him.

   _____

   _____

4. I made up a story about Uncle Tiger and then Uncle Fox chased him and I am sorry for the trick I played.

   _____

   _____

Name _____

# Correct Sentences

**Correct each stringy sentence. Make three simple sentences, or make one simple sentence and one compound sentence. Add punctuation and capital letters where needed.**

1. Rabbit loved to brag and Turtle loved to boast and this caused an argument.

   _____

   _____

2. Turtle and Rabbit decided to race and Rabbit was certain of winning and so he gave Turtle a lead.

   _____

   _____

3. All the animals gathered for the race and some were at the starting point and others were at the end.

   _____

   _____

4. Rabbit jumped quickly to the top of the first ridge and he saw that Turtle was far ahead and so Rabbit ran even faster.

   _____

   _____

5. Turtle tricked Rabbit and then Rabbit lost the race and Turtle kept his secret to himself.

   _____

   _____

# More Singular/Plural Nouns

**Read this script from Trickster TV Talk Show. Use proofreading marks to correct the ten errors in capitalization, end punctuation, and the spelling of plural nouns.**

### Proofreading Marks

| | |
|---|---|
| ⊓ | Indent |
| ∧ | Add |
| ℘ | Delete |
| ≡ | Capital letter |
| / | Small letter |
| ⊙ | Add Period |
| ∧ | Add Comma |
| ˇˇ | Add Quotes |
| ∼ | Transpose |

**Example:** trickster TV brings you great programes?

**HOST:** Today I would like to welcome our friendes Spider and Turtle. Spider, why did you invite Turtle to dinner.

**SPIDER:** He was very hungry

**TURTLE:** I certainly was, but you ate all the food. you left only the dishs.

**HOST:** Is that true?

**SPIDER:** I offered Turtle some berrys, but he left the table.

**TURTLE:** what an unhappy time I had?

**HOST:** Our program for today is over. Tomorrow our guestes will be Aunt Fox and Uncle Fox. We will talk about frying fish and baking loafs of bread.

Name _____

# Trickster Story Map

| Characters and Setting |
| --- |
| The Trickster and Its Character Traits |
| Other Characters |
| The Setting |

| Plot |
| --- |
| The Problem |
| The Trick and the Steps Taken to Carry It Out |
| The Results |

Name _____

# Using Dialogue

Follow these rules when writing dialogue:

► Use quotation marks to enclose the spoken
words. Use an end mark before the closing
quotation mark if the sentence ends there.
Rodney Raccoon whispered, "I'm sleepy."

► Use a comma before the closing quotation
mark if the sentence continues.
"I'm sleepy," whispered Rodney Raccoon.

**Rewrite these sentences as dialogue. Use correct punctuation.**

1. Rodney told Ricky that Ricky didn't know how to clean the den.

_____

_____

2. Ricky replied that he could clean better than anyone.

_____

_____

3. Rodney told Ricky to show that he could clean it.

_____

_____

4. Ricky asked Rodney what he needed to do.

_____

_____

5. Rodney replied that he would give Ricky an hour to clean.

_____

_____

Name _____

# Incredible Stories

What do you think makes a story incredible? Is it the characters, the setting, or the events? Complete the web with words or phrases that describe an incredible story.

Incredible
Stories

Now list some books, movies, or real events that you think are incredible.

_____

_____

_____

_____

Name _____

# Incredible Stories

Fill in the chart as you read the stories.

| | What incredible thing happens? | How do the characters respond? |
|---|---|---|
| **Dogzilla** | | |
| **The Mysterious Giant of Barletta** | | |
| **Raising Dragons** | | |
| **The Garden of Abdul Gasazi** | | |

Name _____

# Monster Words

**Circle the two words that are most alike in meaning.**

1. colossal
   small
   big

2. animal
   creature
   tree

3. strong
   brave
   heroic

4. huge
   monstrous
   bad

5. enormous
   terrifying
   scary

6. tremendous
   tiny
   large

7. frightening
   fun
   horrifying

8. little
   tremendous
   colossal

9. terrifying
   horrifying
   monstrous

10. colossal
    heroic
    monstrous

Name _____

# Fantasy and Realism Chart

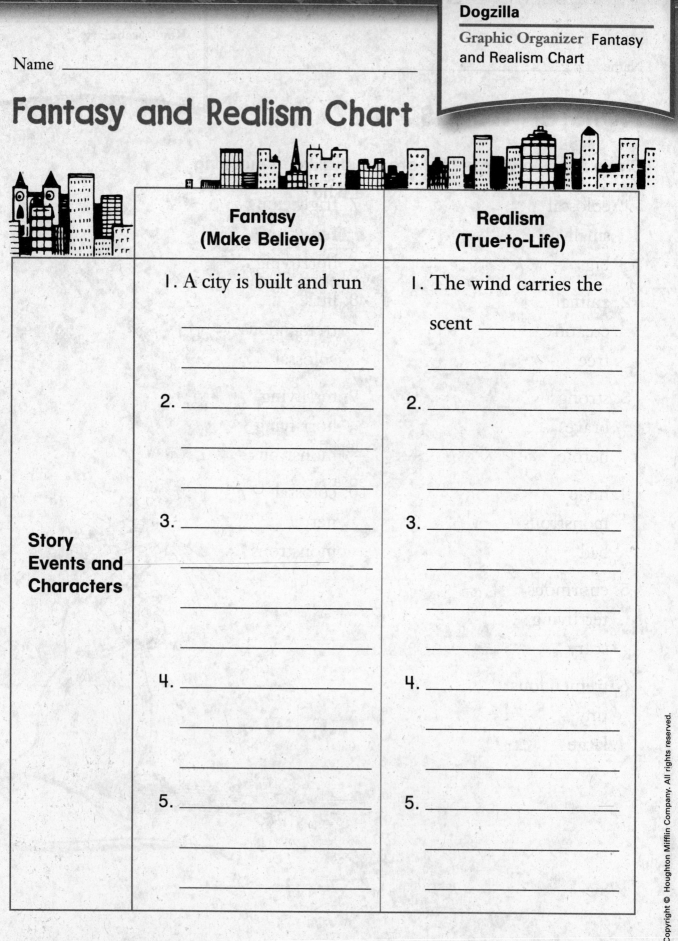

| Story Events and Characters | Fantasy (Make Believe) | Realism (True-to-Life) |
|---|---|---|
| | 1. A city is built and run _____ _____ | 1. The wind carries the scent _____ _____ |
| | 2. _____ _____ _____ | 2. _____ _____ _____ |
| | 3. _____ _____ _____ | 3. _____ _____ _____ |
| | 4. _____ _____ _____ | 4. _____ _____ _____ |
| | 5. _____ _____ _____ | 5. _____ _____ _____ |

Name _____

# Fix the Facts

**Read this newspaper story about *Dogzilla*, and draw a line through the mistakes. Then write what really happened.**

## Monster Makes News!

The people in Mousopolis took part in a Cook-Off. It was winter, and smoke lifted over the city. Soon a strange sound was heard: "Quack . . . quack." Then Dogzilla climbed out of a cave!

The troops were sent out. But Dogzilla hid, and the troops danced home. Dogzilla wandered the city looking for a place to sleep. The mice called a meeting. The mice decided the only way to defeat Dogzilla was to think like a donkey. So they munched grass and waited. It worked! Dogzilla ran out of town. And the problem was solved forever.

_____

_____

_____

_____

_____

_____

Name _____

# A Real Fantasy

**Read the story.  Find parts that are fantasy
and parts that could happen in real life.**

## A Fish Tale

Way up north, it's cold and dark for much of the year.
But that's how polar bears like it, or at least, that's what
people think.

"I hate the cold and dark," said Ursa Bear from her seat by
the fire.  "I want to go where it's warm!"

"That's silly!" snapped her sister.  "Now go catch some
fish for dinner."

Soon Ursa sat by the ocean's edge, waiting.  Her first catch
was a mackerel with shiny scales.

"Please don't eat me," begged the fish.  "If you let me go,
I'll grant you one wish!"

"Can you do that?" asked Ursa.  "Then I wish I were
somewhere sunny and warm!  Here, my friend, I'll let you go."

At once Ursa found herself on a sunny beach next to some
surprised people.  "This is great!" she cried.  "Now where can I
find a beach chair?"

The mackerel was even happier.  "That's the tenth bear
I've wished away today!" he laughed.  "Soon my fish friends
and I will be all by ourselves."

Name _____

# A Real Fantasy continued

**Finish the chart. List five fantasy details and five realistic details from the story.**

| Fantasy Details (make-believe) | Realistic Details (true-to-life) |
|---|---|
| 1. _____ _____ | 1. _____ _____ |
| 2. _____ _____ | 2. _____ _____ |
| 3. _____ _____ | 3. _____ _____ |
| 4. _____ _____ | 4. _____ _____ |
| 5. _____ _____ | 5. _____ _____ |

**Dogzilla**

Structural Analysis Forming
Plurals of Nouns Ending in
*f* or *fe*

Name _____

# Plurals Puzzle

**Write the plural noun that matches each clue in the puzzle.
Use the Word Bank and a dictionary for help.**

**Word Bank**

| thief | cliff | life | safe | wolf |
|-------|-------|------|------|------|
| wife | calf | shelf | belief | half |

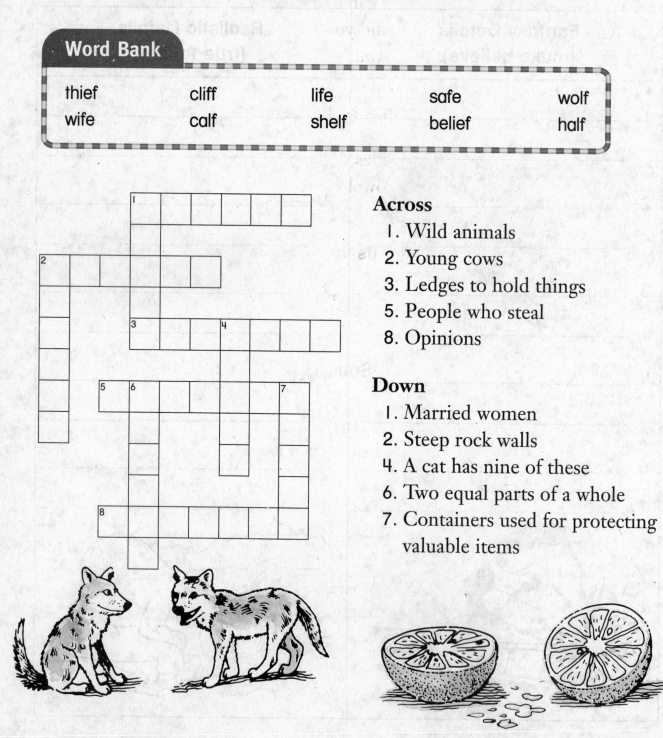

## Across

1. Wild animals
2. Young cows
3. Ledges to hold things
5. People who steal
8. Opinions

## Down

1. Married women
2. Steep rock walls
4. A cat has nine of these
6. Two equal parts of a whole
7. Containers used for protecting valuable items

Name _____

# The Vowel Sounds in *clown* and *lawn*

The /ou/ sound you hear in *clown* can be spelled with
the pattern *ow* or *ou*. The /ô/ sound you hear in *lawn*
can be spelled with these patterns: *aw*, *o*, or *a* before *l*.

/ou/ cl**ow**n, s**ou**nd

/ô/ l**aw**n, cl**o**th, t**a**lk

▶ In the starred word *would*, *ou* does not spell the /ou/
sound. Instead, *ou* spells the vowel sound you hear
in the word *book*.

**Write each Spelling Word under its vowel sound.**

1. clown
2. lawn
3. talk
4. sound
5. cloth
6. would*
7. also
8. mouth
9. crown
10. soft
11. count
12. law

**/ou/ Sound**                    **/ô/ Sound**

_____          _____

_____          _____

_____          _____

_____          _____

_____          _____

**Another Vowel Sound**

_____

# Spelling Spree

**Hidden Words** Write the Spelling Word that is
hidden in each group of letters. Do not let the
other letters fool you.

**Example**: e t i t o w n p e   *town*

1. p r e s o f t a c _____

2. c h a l s o g h e r _____

3. l a n r c l o t h _____

4. r e c l o w n e f _____

**Letter Swap** Change the underlined letter in each
word to make a Spelling Word. Write the Spelling
Word.

**Example**: sh<u>a</u>ll *small*

5. cour<u>t</u> _____     9. tal<u>l</u> _____

6. <u>d</u>awn _____     10. wor<u>l</u>d _____

7. crow<u>s</u> _____     11. l<u>o</u>w _____

8. <u>s</u>outh _____     12. <u>m</u>ound _____

Name _____

# Proofreading and Writing

**Proofreading** Circle the five misspelled Spelling Words. Then write each word correctly.

Spelling Words

## WARNING TO MICE!

The monster has had puppies! At last cownt, six had been seen. They are now in the city. Do not think of these dogs as sawft and cute. They tore up a laun! They chewed up some kloth! Many mice woud fit in one puppy's mouth. So if you see one, run!

**Spelling Words**

1. clown
2. lawn
3. talk
4. sound
5. cloth
6. would*
7. also
8. mouth
9. crown
10. soft
11. count
12. law

1. _____    4. _____

2. _____    5. _____

3. _____

**Write a Comparison** How big is a mouse? How big is a dog? What does a mouse eat? What does a dog eat? How many feet does each animal have? What are their tails like?

**On a separate piece of paper, write a comparison of a dog and a mouse. Tell how they are alike and how they are different. Use Spelling Words from the list.**

Name _____

# Find Meaning Using Context

**Choose the correct definition for each of the
underlined words in the passage. Write the letter
of the definition after the number of the word it
matches. Use context clues to help you.**

a. ran away, fled

b. frightened, alarmed

c. helpful, constructive

d. enjoyment, pleasure

e. shiver or shake

f. relating to a very
early time before
events were written
down

g. carved, as a design
on metal or glass

h. very bad, terrible

i. extremely deep place

j. call forth, gather
together

All at once, the volcano began to <u>tremble</u> and rumble. Up
from the <u>depths</u> of the earth came the <u>dreadful</u> Dogzilla! This

<small>1</small>                   2               3

monster was millions of years old, from <u>prehistoric</u> times. The

<small>4</small>

mice didn't think they could teach it to do anything <u>positive</u> for

<small>5</small>

their town. Using all the courage they could <u>muster</u>, the mice

<small>6</small>

approached Dogzilla. They hit her with a blast of warm, sudsy

water. The <u>panicking</u> pooch took off at <u>top speed</u>. Delighted,

<small>7</small>

the Big Cheese watched with <u>relish</u> as Dogzilla <u>hightailed</u> it

<small>8</small>                   9

out of town. The scary memory of the bubble bath was <u>etched</u>

<small>10</small>

in Dogzilla's mind forever.

1. _____        4. _____        7. _____

2. _____        5. _____        8. _____        10. _____

3. _____        6. _____        9. _____

Name _____

# Writing Possessive Nouns

**Rewrite each phrase, using a possessive.**

1. the barbecue of the mouse

_____

2. the behavior of the animal

_____

3. the barbecue of the mice

_____

4. the shouts of the mayor

_____

5. the smoke of two volcanoes

_____

6. the shouts of the citizens

_____

7. the tail of the cat

_____

8. the cries of the soldiers

_____

9. the dog belonging to the Smiths

_____

10. the dog belonging to Abigail

_____

Name _____

# Finding the Possessive

On the line provided, write the noun in parentheses
as a possessive noun to complete each sentence.
Then write *S* if the possessive noun is singular, and
*P* if it is plural.

1. The _____ pictures dazzle the
   reader. (artist) ___

2. I think that the _____ interest
   will be high. (readers) ___

3. An _____ imagination is clear
   on every page. (illustrator) ___

4. The _____ expression looks
   like a smile. (dog) ___

5. At the end of the story, the _____
   faces are adorable. (puppies) ___

6. Most _____ faces aren't that
   cute! (monsters) ___

7. Every _____ reaction will be a
   little different. (reader) ___

8. All of the _____ actions were
   ridiculous. (characters) ___

9. I think that our _____ favorite
   character is Dogzilla. (class) ___

10. The book was awarded a prize by the _____
    committee. (teachers) ___

Name _____

# Apostrophes

**Rewrite each of the following sentences, adding apostrophes to each incorrectly spelled possessive noun.**

1. How would Dav Pilkeys book be different if it were called *Frogzilla*?

_____

_____

2. The city would be crushed by Frogzillas huge feet.

_____

_____

3. The new heros name might be Dennis the Fly.

_____

_____

4. What do you think the flys strategy would be?

_____

_____

5. What are the frogs weaknesses?

_____

_____

Name _____

# Writing a Journal Entry

In the space below, write a journal entry for today.
Describe things you see, feel, think about, or remember.
Then use your entry to complete the table below.

## My Daily Journal

**Today's Date:** _____

_____

_____

_____

_____

_____

_____

_____

_____

### What I Wrote About Today

| Facts | Observations | Feelings | Memories | Ideas |
|-------|--------------|----------|----------|-------|
|       |              |          |          |       |
|       |              |          |          |       |
|       |              |          |          |       |

Name _____

# Voice

Suppose one of the puppies wrote this journal entry:

Those silly mice!  They think their big barbecue tommorow will
go off without a hitch.  Well, they've had their peace and quiet.
Now let's see if they like to play with puppys!  I'm raring to go,
and I'm planning on having lots of fun in Mousopolis tomorrow.
And if they tries any of that bath stuff on me, we'll just see who
can take a licking!

Suppose the Big Cheese wrote this in his journal:

Tomorrow is the first anniversary of the Dogzilla disaster, and
that makes me nervous.  What hapened to Dogzilla?  Can we be
sure she don't come back?  Will tomorrow be the day a new
monster destroies poor Mousopolis yet again?  I'm scared!

1. How would you describe the puppy's voice in his entry?

   _____

   _____

2. How would you describe the Big Cheese's voice in his entry?

   _____

   _____

**In both journal entries, circle examples of grammar and
spelling that are not perfect.**

# Revising Your Story

**Reread your story. Put a checkmark in the box for each sentence that describes your paper. Use this page to help you revise.**

## Rings the Bell

☐ My story has a beginning, a middle, and an ending. It is focused on a clear problem.

☐ Many details tell about the characters and setting.

☐ Exact words make a clear picture for the reader.

☐ I wrote in a way that will get my readers' attention.

☐ Sentences flow well. There are few mistakes.

## Getting Stronger

☐ The beginning or ending is confusing. The problem is unclear.

☐ I need more details about my characters and my setting.

☐ More exact words are needed.

☐ My writing doesn't always hold my readers' attention.

☐ Some sentences are choppy. There are some mistakes.

## Try Harder

☐ There is no beginning, middle, or ending. There is no problem.

☐ I didn't use any details.

☐ There are no exact words. I used the same word many times.

☐ I can't hear my voice at all. My readers might be bored.

☐ Most sentences are choppy. Mistakes make it hard to read.

Name _____

# Using Possessive Nouns

A **possessive noun** shows ownership.
► Add **'s** to make a noun possessive.
► Add just an **'** (apostrophe) to make a plural
   noun that ends with *s* a possessive noun.

**Rewrite each phrase, using a possessive noun. Then use
the new phrase in a sentence of your own.**

1. the equipment of the team _____

   _____

   _____

2. the teamwork of the players _____

   _____

   _____

3. the orders of the coach _____

   _____

   _____

4. the roar of the audience _____

   _____

   _____

5. the songs of the cheerleaders _____

   _____

   _____

Name _____

# Spelling Words

Look for spelling patterns you have learned to help you remember the Spelling Words on this page. Think about the parts that you find hard to spell.

**Write the missing letters in the Spelling Words below.**

1. an _____
2. s _____ _____ d
3. go _____ _____
4. go _____ _____ _____
5. s _____ me
6. som _____ thing
7. y _____ _____
8. y _____ _____ _____
9. fr _____ _____ nd
10. s _____ _____ ool
11. w _____ ere
12. m _____ _____ elf

**Study List** On another sheet of paper, write each Spelling Word. Check the list to be sure you spell each word correctly.

Name _____

# Spelling Spree

**The Third Word** Write the Spelling Word that belongs in each group.

1. I, me, _____

2. plus, also, _____

3. talked, spoke, _____

4. pal, buddy, _____

5. their, our, _____

6. moves, runs, _____

**Sentence Fillers** Write the Spelling Word that makes the most sense in each sentence below.

7. Do you know _____ soccer practice is tomorrow?

8. I have _____ books about bears that I bought last summer.

9. Our _____ usually lets out at 3 o'clock.

10. When is your class _____ to the library?

11. My brother wrote _____ in my notebook, but I can't read it.

12. Have _____ seen my pet snake anywhere?

**Spelling Words**

1. and
2. said
3. goes
4. going
5. some
6. something
7. you
8. your
9. friend
10. school
11. where
12. myself

Theme 3: **Incredible Stories** 213

Name _____

# Proofreading and Writing

**Proofreading** Circle the four misspelled Spelling Words in the story. Then write each word correctly.

**Spelling Words**

1. and
2. said
3. goes
4. going
5. some
6. something
7. you
8. your
9. friend
10. school
11. where
12. myself

Yesterday, I was on my way into skool when I heard something rustling in the bushes. I turned around an went over to see what it was. I looked in the spot were I had heard the noise, but there was nothing there. Then, from behind me, a voice sed, "Are you looking for me?" I turned around and found myself face to face with a fox with a sly grin on its face.

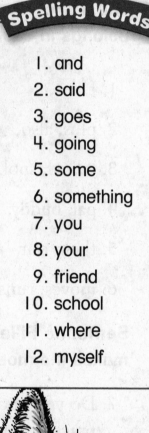

1. _____  3. _____

2. _____  4. _____

**Incredible Sentences** Write four sentences that tell about something incredible. Use a Spelling Word from the list in each one.

Name _____

# What Do These Words Mean?

**Look up each word in your glossary. Then, in the box above each word, draw a picture that shows the meaning of the word.**

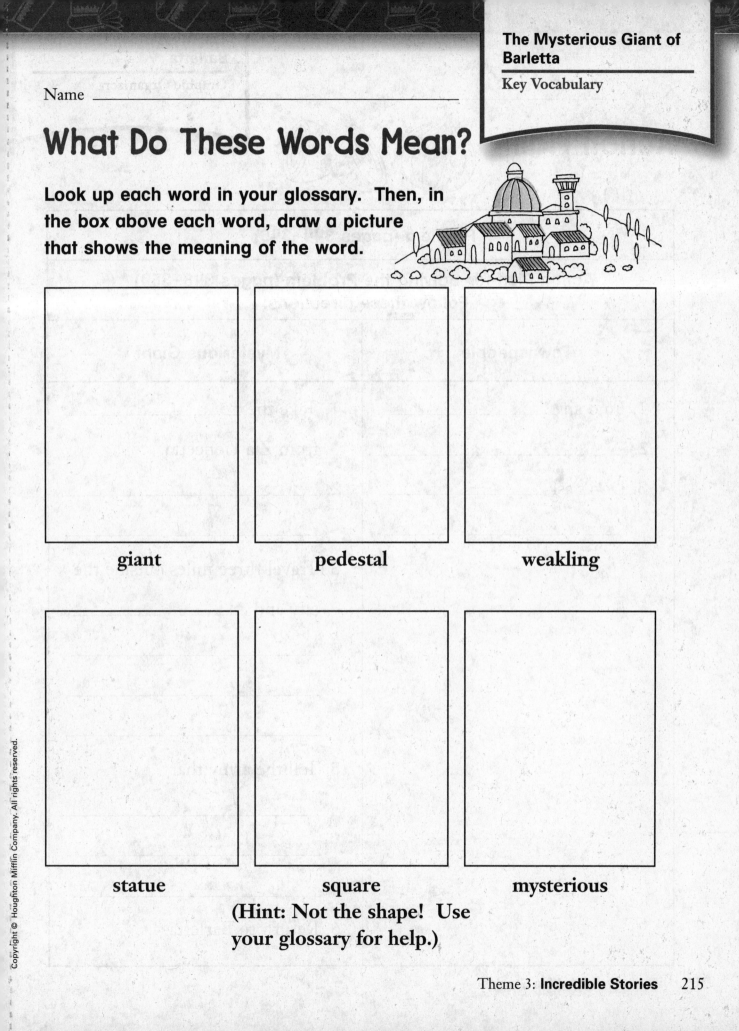

|  |  |  |
|---|---|---|
| giant | pedestal | weakling |

| statue | square | mysterious |
|---|---|---|

**(Hint: Not the shape! Use your glossary for help.)**

Name _____

# Action Plan

| Problem (pages 344–345) |
|---|

| Action Plan for Solving the Problem (pages 348–354) Follow these directions: |
|---|

| **Townspeople** | **Mysterious Giant** |
|---|---|
| 1. Find an _____. | 1. Take the _____ from Zia Concetta. |
| 2. _____ | 2. _____ |
| 3. Don't ask _____ _____. | 3. Travel three miles outside the city and _____. |
| | 4. _____ _____ _____ |
| | 5. Tell the army that _____ _____ _____ |
| | 6. Return to Barletta. |

Name _____

# Remember the Details

**Think about *The Mysterious Giant of Barletta*. Then complete the sentences.**

1. The people of Barletta show their love for the Mysterious Giant by

   _____

   _____

2. The peaceful time for Barletta is over when

   _____

   _____

3. Zia Concetta and the Giant figure out a plan to save Barletta. The plan is

   _____

   _____

4. After the soldiers hear what the Giant says, they wonder

   _____

   _____

5. The army captain decides there is only one thing to do, so they

   _____

   _____

Name _____

# Directions for Fun

**Read the directions. Then answer the questions on the next page.**

### Fingertip Puppets

Act out your favorite folktale or story using puppets you've made yourself. It's easy and fun to do. All you need are an old rubber glove, scissors, glue, marking pens, and some craft supplies.

First, find an old rubber glove that can be cut apart. Each finger will become a puppet. Draw a line about 2 ½ inches below each fingertip of the glove. Cut along the line and then turn the fingertip inside out.

Next, make the puppet look special. Draw a funny face on your puppet. Then glue on hair made from cotton or yarn. Finally, glue on a hat, shirt, or collar made with pieces of felt. You may also want to add beads, buttons, or trims.

Name _____

# Directions for Fun continued

**Answer each question about making a fingertip puppet.**

1. What supplies will you need?

   _____

   _____

2. After you find an old rubber glove, what do you do?

   _____

   _____

3. Why should you draw the line before you cut?

   _____

   _____

4. After you cut off the fingertip, what should you do next?

   _____

   _____

5. What should you do before you glue on the hair?

   _____

   _____

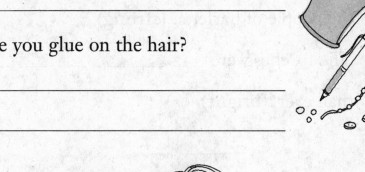

Name _____

# Giant Endings

**Fill in each blank using the base word and the ending *-er* or *-est*. The base words are in dark type. To solve the puzzle, write the numbered letter from each answer on the line with the matching number.**

1. The statue was the __ __ __ __ __ __ __ thing
   in Barletta. **(tall)**
   <sub>5</sub>

2. The statue had been in the square __ __ __ __ __ __
   than anyone could remember. **(long)**
   <sub>7</sub>

3. To the Giant, late nights were the __ __ __ __ __ __
   time of all. **(nice)**
   <sub>1</sub>

4. The town was __ __ __ __ __ __ __ at night
   than at any other time. **(quiet)**
   <sub>3</sub>

5. The army was __ __ __ __ __ __ __ than
   the people of Barletta. **(strong)**
   <sub>2</sub>  <sub>6</sub>

6. The torches were __ __ __ __ __ __ __ __
   than ever. **(bright)**
   <sub>4</sub>

The Mysterious Giant has a lot of:

__ __ __ __ __ __ __
1  2  3  4  5  6  7

Name _____

# Vowel + /r/ Sounds

**Remember these spelling patterns for the vowel + /r/ sounds:**

| Patterns | | Examples |
|---|---|---|
| /är/ | **ar** | dark |
| /îr/ | **ear** | clear |
| /ôr/ | **or** | north |
| /ûr/ | **er** | her |
| | **ir** | girl |
| | **ur** | turn |
| | **or** | work |

**Write each Spelling Word under its vowel + /r/ sounds.**

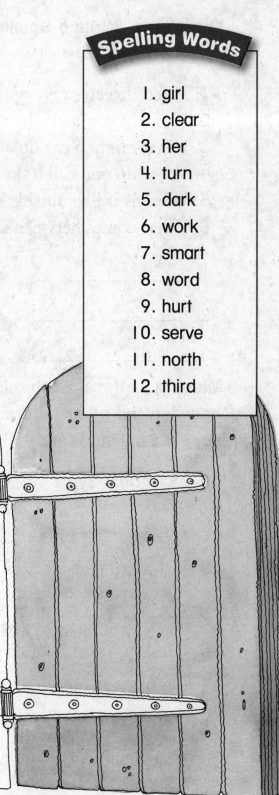

**/är/ Sounds**

_____

_____

**/îr/ Sounds**

_____

_____

**/ôr/ Sounds**

_____

**/ûr/ Sounds**

_____

_____

_____

_____

_____

## Spelling Words

1. girl
2. clear
3. her
4. turn
5. dark
6. work
7. smart
8. word
9. hurt
10. serve
11. north
12. third

Name _____

# Spelling Spree

**Questions** Write a Spelling Word to answer each question.

1. What direction is opposite to south?
2. How do you feel when you solve a hard problem?
3. What might a car do at a street corner?
4. What do you call a sky without clouds?
5. What is it like outside after sunset?
6. What comes between second and fourth?

1. _____    4. _____

2. _____    5. _____

3. _____    6. _____

**Missing Letters** Each missing letter fits in ABC order between the other letters. Write the missing letters to spell a Spelling Word.

**Example:** g __ i   n __ p   q __ s   m __ o   *horn*

7. r __ t   d __ f   q __ s   u __ w   d __ f   _____

8. g __ i   d __ f   q __ s   _____

9. v __ x   n __ p   q __ s   j __ l   _____

10. f __ h   h __ j   q __ s   k __ m   _____

11. v __ x   n __ p   q __ s   c __ e   _____

12. g __ i   t __ v   q __ s   s __ u   _____

Name _____

# Proofreading and Writing

**Proofreading** **Circle the four misspelled Spelling Words below. Then write each word correctly.**

Here is a good way to reach Barletta.
Head noarth from Naples. At the edge of
town, turn right onto the main highway. This
road should be pretty cleer. Take the therd exit
after you reach the coast. You should get to
Barletta before darck.

**Spelling Words**

1. girl
2. clear
3. her
4. turn
5. dark
6. work
7. smart
8. word
9. hurt
10. serve
11. north
12. third

_____   _____

_____   _____

**Write a Description** If you were to make a statue, who would
be your subject? Where would it stand so others could see it?

**On a separate sheet of paper, write a description of your
statue. Tell where it will be placed. Use Spelling Words
from the list.**

# Which Meaning Is Correct?

**From the definitions below, choose the correct meaning for the underlined word in each sentence. Write the number of the meaning in the blank provided.**

---

**bargain** *noun* **1.** An agreement between two sides; deal: *We made a bargain to split the chores.* **2.** Something offered or bought at a low price: *The book was a bargain at 25 cents.*

---

**hail** *verb* **1.** To greet or welcome by calling out: *We hailed our friends as they got off the bus.* **2.** To call or signal to: *I hailed a taxi at the corner* **3.** To congratulate by cheering: *The crowd hailed the hero's return.*

---

**settle** *verb* **1.** To arrange or decide upon: *Let's settle the argument today.* **2.** To come to rest: *The leaf settled on the grass.* **3.** To make a home or place to live in: *Pioneers settled on the prairie.*

---

1. Every day, the townspeople <u>hailed</u> the Mysterious Giant as they walked to the market. _____

2. They asked the statue to help them find a good <u>bargain</u> at the market. _____

3. Doves flew to the statue and <u>settled</u> on his head. _____

4. The Mysterious Giant was <u>hailed</u> as a hero. _____

Name _____

# Circling Verbs

**Circle the verb in each sentence.**

1. The giant statue stands in the center of town.

2. People often look at the statue.

3. Everyone loves the statue.

4. Zia Concetta is the oldest person in Barletta.

5. One day, an enemy army approaches the town.

6. Everyone fears the army of powerful soldiers.

7. The soldiers march toward the town.

8. The mysterious statue hops off his pedestal.

9. He asks for three special things.

10. The giant statue cries because of the onion's smell.

# Finding Verbs

**Find the verb in each sentence, and write it on the line at the right.**

1. In this story, the giant statue leaps off its pedestal. _____

2. The people believe in the giant. _____

3. Clearly, the giant cares about the town of Barletta. _____

4. Unfortunately, an army attacks the town. _____

5. The people quickly identify the trouble. _____

6. With a little thought, the giant solves the problem. _____

7. He cuts an onion into two pieces. _____

8. The tears run down his face. _____

9. The army fears the giant and his friends. _____

10. At the end of the story, the soldiers leave town. _____

**Use this chart to classify the verbs from the sentences above.**

| Physical Action | Mental Action |
|---|---|
| _____ | _____ |
| _____ | _____ |
| _____ | _____ |
| _____ | _____ |
| _____ | _____ |

Name _____

# Using Exact Verbs

**Circle the verb in each sentence. Then think of an
exact verb to make the sentence more interesting.
Rewrite the sentence using your exact verb.**

1. An army of powerful soldiers appears.

_____

2. One night, Zia Concetta goes to the statue.

_____

3. The giant statue moves off the pedestal.

_____

4. The statue's clever plan beats the large army.

_____

5. Today, the statue still is in Barletta, Italy.

_____

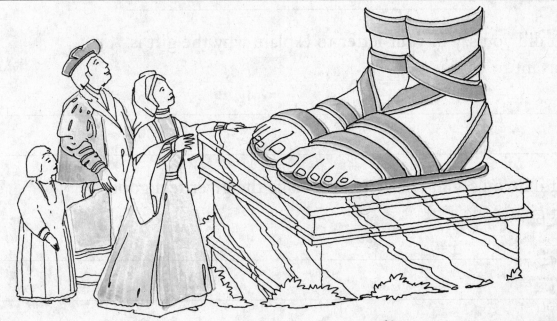

Theme 3: **Incredible Stories**     227

Name _____

# Write a Thank-You Note

**Use this outline to write a thank-you letter for a gift you have been given. When you have finished your letter, answer the questions below.**

Address/Date _____
_____
_____

Greeting _____

Body _____
_____
_____
_____

Closing _____

Signature _____

What did you say in your letter to explain why the gift is important to you?

_____

_____

What did you say in your letter to make the giver feel good about giving the gift?

_____

_____

Name _____

# Using Commas for Direct Address

What if in all the excitement at Barletta, no one remembered to thank the vegetable store owner for supplying the very important onion?

**Suppose that the thank-you note has now been written, but it needs proofreading. Read the note. Add commas where they belong, before or after the name of the person being addressed.**

Dear Sir,

    We the people of Barletta thank you for supplying the onion that made our giant cry! Sir without your onion, our whole plan might have failed miserably. We were ready to run from Barletta, but you Sir stayed bravely in your shop, guarding your vegetables. When your city needed you, you were ready Sir. When we said, "Sir find us an onion," you knew just what to do. Now everyone will always say that it was because of you and your onion that Barletta was saved. Sir you have reason to be proud!

                    Sincerely,
                    The Mayor

Name _____

# Farm Words

**Vocabulary**

appetite

chores

harvested

hitched

plow

sown

tended

**Write each word next to its definition.**

1. gathered or picked _____

2. planted _____

3. hunger _____

4. jobs _____

5. break up and turn over dirt _____

6. took care of _____

7. tied or fastened _____

**Write sentences to answer these questions.**

8. When you have a big appetite, what do you do?

_____

9. What kinds of fruits or vegetables have you harvested?

_____

10. What are your favorite chores? What chores don't you like to do?

_____

Name _____

# Conclusions Chart

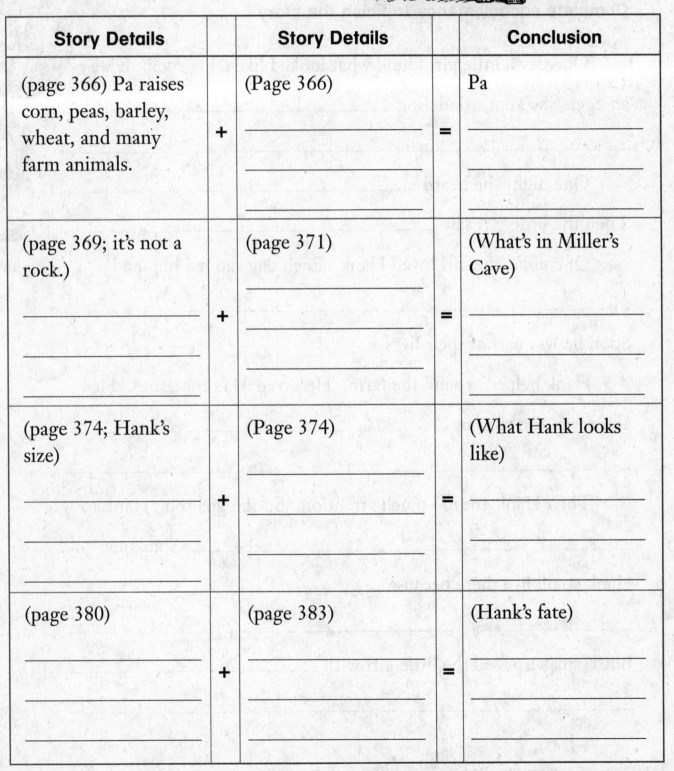

| Story Details | | Story Details | | Conclusion |
|---|---|---|---|---|
| (page 366) Pa raises corn, peas, barley, wheat, and many farm animals. | + | (Page 366) _____ _____ _____ | = | Pa _____ _____ _____ |
| (page 369; it's not a rock.) _____ _____ | + | (page 371) _____ _____ _____ | = | (What's in Miller's Cave) _____ _____ _____ |
| (page 374; Hank's size) _____ _____ _____ | + | (Page 374) _____ _____ _____ | = | (What Hank looks like) _____ _____ _____ |
| (page 380) _____ _____ _____ | + | (page 383) _____ _____ _____ | = | (Hank's fate) _____ _____ _____ |

Name _____

# The Dragon's Tale

**Tell what happened in *Raising Dragons*.**
**Complete each sentence to finish the story.**

One day a little girl found what looked like a big rock.  It was

an egg.  She kept wondering _____

_____.

One night she heard _____.

Then the little girl saw _____.

Of course, the girl loved Hank.  Each day she fed him and

_____.

Soon he was part of their lives.

Hank helped around the farm.  He saved Ma's tomatoes.  He

also saved the corn by _____

_____.

Then Hank got too much attention.  So the girl took Hank to

_____.  She knew

Hank could live there because _____

_____

But Hank surprised the little girl with _____

_____

Name _____

# Conclusions from Clues

**Read these details about dragons. Then fill in the chart on the next page.**

## What Dragons Are Really Like

▶ Dragons have skin much like snakes, lizards, and other reptiles. Since they are cold-blooded, dragons like to live in warm spots.

▶ Each spring, dragons lay eggs in nests they build. Their nests are made from the same materials that birds use.

▶ Dragons can fly, but their wings are not at all like birds' wings. They are more like large, leathery bat wings.

▶ Usually, dragons will not harm people. They only eat frogs, bugs, and fish. Some dragons have been trained to be useful. They pull plows and do other tasks that horses do.

▶ Dragons do not breathe fire. However, their teeth are larger than a shark's, and they will use them to keep their babies safe.

Name _____

# Conclusions from
# Clues continued

**Read each conclusion. Decide if it is correct, and write
YES or NO. Write the clues that helped
you decide.**

| Conclusions | Correct Conclusion? (Yes or No) | Story Clues |
|---|---|---|
| Dragon skin is scaly. | _____ | _____ |
| Dragon nests are made of twigs, sticks, and grasses. | _____ | _____ |
| Dragon wings have feathers. | _____ | _____ _____ |
| Dragons can be trained to carry riders. | _____ | _____ _____ |
| Dragons never bite. | _____ | _____ |

234   Theme 3: **Incredible Stories**

Name _____

# Happy Endings

**Choose a word from the box to match each picture clue.**
**Write the word on the line.**

## Word Bank

| | | | | |
|---|---|---|---|---|
| proudly | brightly | leaky | cloudy | beastly |
| furry | lovely | bumpy | rainy | hairy |

1. + y = ___ ___ ___ ___ ___

2. + ly = ___ ___ ___ ___ ___ ___ ___ ___

3. + y = ___ ___ ___ ___ ___ ___

4. + ly = ___ ___ ___ ___ ___ ___ ___

5. + y = ___ ___ ___ ___ ___

6. + ly = ___ ___ ___ ___ ___ ___

Name _____

# The /j/, /k/, and /kw/ Sounds

▶ The /j/ sound can be spelled with the consonant *j* or with the consonant *g* followed by *e* or *y*.

/j/ **j**eans, lar**ge**, **gy**m

▶ The starred word *judge* has two /j/ sounds in it. The first /j/ sound is spelled *j*, and the second is spelled *dge*.

▶ The /k/ sound can be spelled with *k*, *ck*, or *c*. The /kw/ sounds can be spelled with the *qu* pattern.

/k/ par**k**, qui**ck**, pi**c**ni**c**       /kw/ s**qu**eeze

**Write the Spelling Words that have the /j/ sound in them. Then write the Spelling Words that have the /k/ or /kw/ sounds in them.**

**/j/ Sound**

_____

_____

_____

_____

_____

**/k/ or /kw/ Sounds**

_____

_____

_____

_____

_____

Name _____

# Spelling Spree

**Silly Rhymes** Write a Spelling Word to complete each sentence. The answer rhymes with the underlined word.

1. large
2. gym
3. skin
4. quick
5. picnic
6. judge
7. park
8. jeans
9. crack
10. orange
11. second
12. squeeze

1. The hungry _____ ate some <u>fudge</u>.

2. Birds in the _____ sleep after <u>dark</u>.

3. I dropped baked <u>beans</u> on my new _____ .

4. There is a _____ in the train <u>track</u>.

5. Can more <u>bees</u> _____ into the hive?

6. A _____ <u>barge</u> is on the river.

1. _____     4. _____

2. _____     5. _____

3. _____     6. _____

**Letter Math** Solve each problem by using a Spelling Word.

**Example:** joke – ke + b = *job*

7. pick – k + nic = _____

8. or + angel – l = _____

9. s + king – g = _____     11. sec + fond – f = _____

10. quit – t + ck = _____     12. edgy – ed + m = _____

Name _____

# Proofreading and Writing

**Proofreading** Circle the five misspelled Spelling Words. Then write each word correctly.

Dear Diary,

    Today we went to the zoo. We saw larje snakes and turtles. One turtle splashed water on my geans! There was a dragon cage, but it was empty. I guess the dragons were taking a quik nap inside. For lunch we had a picnick. I ate mine in the parc.

1. large
2. gym
3. skin
4. quick
5. picnic
6. judge
7. park
8. jeans
9. crack
10. orange
11. second
12. squeeze

1. _____

2. _____

3. _____

4. _____

5. _____

**Write a List of Rules** A baby dragon would need a lot of care. What rules should someone follow when raising a dragon?

**On a separate sheet of paper, write a list of rules for taking care of a dragon. Use Spelling Words from the list.**

Name _____

# Say It Right!

| | | | |
|---|---|---|---|
| **Pronunciation Key** | | | |
| ă map | ĭ pit | oi oil | th bath |
| ā pay | ī ride | ŏŏ book | _th_ bathe |
| â care | î fierce | ōō boot | ə ago, item, |
| ä father | ŏ pot | ou out | pencil, atom, |
| ĕ pet | ō go | ŭ cup | circus |
| ē be | ô paw, for | û fur | |

**Look at the vowel sound in the words below.  Then look at
the Pronunciation Key and find the sample word with the
same vowel sound.  Write the word on the line.**

1. **must** (mŭst) _____

2. **dirt** (dûrt) _____

3. **breath** (brĕth) _____

4. **path** (păth) _____

5. **chew** (chōō) _____

6. **self** (sĕlf) _____

7. **dear** (dîr) _____

8. **pair** (pâr) _____

9. **meal** (mēl) _____

10. **stay** (stā) _____

# Looking for the Present

Name _____

**Read each sentence.  Choose the correct verb
form and write it on the line to complete the sentence.**

1. This story _____ about a girl
   and her pet dragon. (tell   tells)

2. The dog _____ when it sees
   the giant egg. (barks   bark)

3. The neighbors _____ the egg
   hatching. (watch   watches)

4. A large claw _____ from inside
   the egg. (appear   appears)

5. The girl _____ the newborn
   dragon. (dry   dries)

6. The strange pet _____ when
   he sees the girl. (smiles   smile)

7. Her parents _____ about owning
   a dragon. (worries   worry)

8. Dragons _____ fire. (breathe   breathes)

9. The dragon _____ with the girl
   on his back. (flies   fly)

10. Clouds _____ the two flying friends.
    (surround  surrounds)

Name _____

# Choosing the Present

**Read each sentence. Then write the correct present-time form of the verb in parentheses.**

1. A smart girl _____ a pet dragon. (raise)

2. The chickens _____ when they see the baby dragon. (cluck)

3. All animals _____ to eat. (need)

4. This dragon _____ on fish, frogs, eels, and insects. (munch)

5. The strange creature _____ to be a good friend. (try)

6. The friends _____ the farm together. (cross)

7. The dragon _____ with daily chores. (help)

8. His hot breath _____ the corn in the field. (pop)

9. Customers _____ the dragon's popcorn. (buy)

10. The girl _____ when the dragon leaves. (cry)

Name _____

# Subject-Verb Agreement

**Proofread these paragraphs. Correct
errors in subject-verb agreement.
Circle verbs that are not in the correct time.
Then rewrite the paragraphs on the lines provided.**

 Benjamin wakes at sunrise. He look outside his apartment
window. At first, he see only the sun. Then he spot five black dots
in the distance. The dots grows bigger and bigger. Suddenly, Ben's
jaw drop wide open. Five big black dragons flies outside his window.

 The dragons calls to Benjamin. "Come fly with us!" they shout.
Benjamin think about it. In a few seconds, he decide. In a flash, he
jump onto one of the dragons. The new friends zooms into the air.
Benjamin laughs and wonder what will happen next.

_____

_____

_____

_____

_____

_____

_____

_____

Name _____

# Planning Your Writing

Use this page to plan your opinion. Then number your reasons or details in the order you will use them.

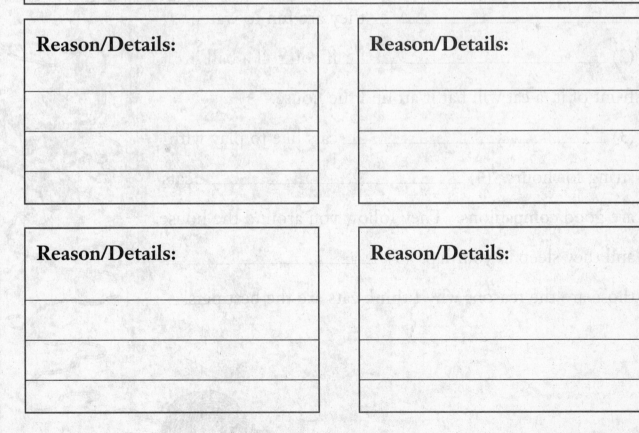

**Topic:** _____

_____

**Topic Sentence:** _____

_____

**Reason/Details:**

**Reason/Details:**

**Reason/Details:**

**Reason/Details:**

Theme 3: **Incredible Stories**      243

Name _____

# Using Commas with Introductory Phrases

**Select the introductory group of words from
the box that best completes each sentence.**

> for example        first of all            in addition
> in conclusion       most important

## Cats Are the Best Pets

I think cats are the best pets.  (1)

_____ they are fun to watch.

(2) _____ if you roll a ball in

front of it, a cat will bat it around the house.

(3) _____ cats like to play with

string for hours.  (4) _____ cats

are good companions.  They follow you around the house,

and they sleep in your lap.  (5) _____

those are the reasons why I think cats are the best pets!

Name _____

# A Garden of Words

**Circle the word that best completes each sentence.
Then write the word in the blank.**

1. The elephants were so large they were _____ .
   A. impossible      C. awesome
   B. weak            D. smart

2. My teacher _____ me that some
   kinds of plants can eat insects.
   A. discovered      C. rewarded
   B. disappeared     D. convinced

3. I saw a bird in a tree, but it flew off and _____ .
   A. disappeared     C. grew
   B. discovered      D. walked

4. In the pond, I _____ a frog that
   looked like a leaf.
   A. thought         C. convinced
   B. discovered      D. read

5. We thought the lion's loud roar was _____ .
   A. quiet           C. incredible
   B. tiny            D. impossible

6. It was almost _____ to see

   the white polar bear sitting in the white snow.
   A. best            C. incredible
   B. awesome         D. impossible

Name _____

# Story Map

## The Garden of Abdul Gasazi

| Characters | Setting |
|---|---|
|  |  |

### Plot

**Problem**

**What Happens**

**Ending**

Name _____

# Mr. Gasazi's Garden!

**Complete each sentence with an event from**
*The Garden of Abdul Gasazi.* **Then explain how**
**you feel about the way the story ends.**

1. Miss Hester must visit Cousin Eunice, so she asks

_____

2. When Alan takes Fritz for a walk,

_____

3. As Alan searches for Fritz, he finds _____

4. The magician tells Alan that he has _____

_____

5. As Alan leaves, _____

6. When Alan returns to Miss Hester's, Fritz _____

_____

7. Miss Hester tells Alan that _____

8. After Alan leaves, Miss Hester tells Fritz that he is a bad dog

because _____

### My Feelings About the Ending:

_____

_____

Name _____

# The Shape of a Story

**Read the story below.**

## Rescuing Dolly

One cold morning as Keisha walked her dog, Vista, she noticed fresh tracks in the snow. A minute later, a small, spotted dog appeared by the river. With no tag or collar, it clearly was lost. It stared hopefully at Keisha and shivered in the cold. Then Vista barked, and the dog ran off. "It's much too cold for a dog to stay outside for long," Keisha thought. "I've got to do something, but Vista will keep scaring it away."

So Keisha headed for home. She told her mother about the lost dog, and together they returned to the river to find it.

Keisha was almost ready to give up, but at last she spotted the dog. Keisha called to it, but it jumped onto a rock. Then Keisha knelt down. The little dog leaped into her arms and began licking her face.

Weeks later, the little dog's owner still could not be found. So that is how Dolly, the little dog, came to be part of Keisha's family.

# The Shape of a Story continued

**Fill in this story map with details from "Rescuing Dolly."**

| Characters | Setting |
|---|---|
| 1. _____ | _____ |
| 2. _____ | |

| Plot |
|---|
| **Problem** |
| _____ |
| **What Happens** |
| 1. _____ |
| 2. _____ |
| 3. _____ |
| 4. _____ |
| **Ending** |
| 1. _____ |
| 2. _____ |

Name _____

# Playing with Prefixes

On each line, write a word that begins with the
prefix *un-*, *dis-*, or *non-* and matches the definition.
Then find and circle all eight words in the word search.

1. not locked _____

2. not fiction _____

3. the opposite of agree _____

4. not able _____

5. the opposite of appear _____

6. not usual _____

7. not fair _____

8. not making sense _____

```
K N O N F I C T I O N D A D F P E P
D E R W H Y N E Z G Q J X H G H T V
I Z W U C Q X U S Y C Y S S V M Z C
S T V A N L N O N S E N S E Z P G Z
A N P K A L M B S U I G I V K A O R
P V N O W J O O D G S P H Q M H M Z
P T G J G Z O C R S S U U N F A I R
E R Y X W L P F K X M P A Z H Z A R
A H E R J Q M W M E G V T L M O J E
R E U N A B L E L P D I S A G R E E
```

Name _____

# Homophones

**Homophones** are words that sound the same but have different spellings and meanings. When you spell a homophone, think about the meaning of the word you want to write.

| **Homophone** | **Meaning** |
|---|---|
| /nōō/ new | not old |
| /nōō/ knew | understood |

**Spelling Words**

1. hear
2. here
3. new
4. knew
5. its
6. it's
7. our
8. hour
9. there
10. their
11. they're

**Write the four pairs of Spelling Words that are homophones.**

_____    _____

_____    _____

_____    _____

_____    _____

**Now write the three Spelling Words that are homophones.**

_____

_____

_____

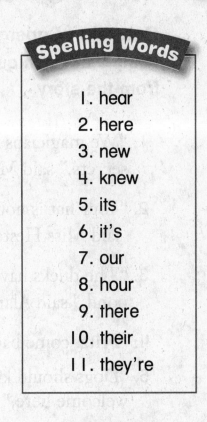

Name _____

# Spelling Spree

**Quotation Caper** **Write the Spelling Word that best completes each quotation that might have come from the story.**

1. "We magicians never reveal _____ secrets," said Mr. Gasazi.

2. "Your hat is not in _____ usual place," said Miss Hester.

3. "The ducks have flown back to _____ pond," said Alan.

4. "Fritz, come back _____ !" called Alan.

5. "Dogs should know that _____ not welcome here," grumbled Gasazi.

1. _____    4. _____

2. _____    5. _____

3. _____

**In Another Word** **Write a Spelling Word to replace each expression.**

6. get wind of        _____

7. hot off the press  _____

8. over yonder        _____

9. got the picture    _____

Name _____

# Proofreading and Writing

**Proofreading** Suppose that Alan keeps a journal.
Circle the five misspelled Spelling Words
in this entry. Then write each word correctly.

**June 3:** Today I had a strange adventure. It was in a
magician's garden. Miss Hester's dog Fritz ran in their.
I knue we were in trouble when I read the sign: "No dogs
allowed." I chased Fritz for at least an our. I think its'
possible that the magician turned Fritz into a duck!
When I came back heere, no one believed my story.

**Spelling Words**

1. hear
2. here
3. new
4. knew
5. its
6. it's
7. our
8. hour
9. there
10. their
11. they're

1. _____

2. _____

3. _____

4. _____

5. _____

**Write a Plan** Abdul Gasazi had some amazing trees
in his garden. If you could plan a garden, what would
you plant in it? Where would you plant things?

**On a separate sheet of paper, draw a picture of your
garden. Then write a plan for it. Tell what you
would plant, and where. Use Spelling Words from
the list.**

grass

pool

Trees

Name _____

# Ask Your Friendly Thesaurus!

**For each underlined word in the following sentences, choose a better word or words from the thesaurus entry. Write your answers in the blanks provided. Some words may have more than one answer.**

## Thesaurus Entries

1. **funny:** silly, unusual, curious, laughable
2. **pulled:** strained, dragged, stretched, heaved
3. **ran:** darted, flowed, fled, hurried
4. **tired:** exhausted, faint, worn, wilting
5. **walking:** strolling, trotting, striding, stomping
6. **shouted:** called, bellowed, howled, bawled

1. Fritz stopped chewing the furniture and fell asleep,

   completely <u>tired</u>. _____

2. Alan fastened Fritz's leash and the dog <u>pulled</u> him out of

   the house. _____

3. Fritz <u>ran</u> straight through the open door.

   _____

4. Gasazi <u>shouted</u> that he had turned the dogs into ducks!

   _____

5. Alan felt <u>funny</u> when he thought the magician had fooled

   him. _____

6. Fritz came <u>walking</u> up the front steps with Alan's hat.

   _____

Name 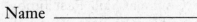 _____

# Choosing Time

**Choose the correct verb form in parentheses and
write it on the line provided to complete the sentence.**

1. Tomorrow Alan _____ Fritz for
   a walk. (takes     will take)

2. Yesterday Alan _____ for Fritz.
   (searched     will search)

3. Yesterday in the garden, Fritz _____
   into Abdul. (bumped     will bump)

4. Tomorrow Alan _____ the stairs.
   (climbed     will climb)

5. Yesterday the ducks _____

   their wings. (flapped     will flap)

**Complete the chart by supplying past and
future time for each of the verbs given.**

| Verb | Past Time | Future Time |
|------|-----------|-------------|
| try | _____ | _____ |
| race | _____ | _____ |
| disappear | _____ | _____ |
| drag | _____ | _____ |
| bolt | _____ | _____ |

Name _____

# Writing Past and Future

**Read each sentence. Then write the
sentence in past time and future time.**

1. Alan walks Fritz.

   **Past:** _____

   **Future:** _____

2. He hurries after the dog.

   **Past:** _____

   **Future:** _____

3. Alan discovers the magician.

   **Past:** _____

   **Future:** _____

4. Abdul shows Alan a duck.

   **Past:** _____

   **Future:** _____

5. The duck grabs Alan's hat.

   **Past:** _____

   **Future:** _____

Name _____

# Keeping Verbs Consistent

**Read this story. The paragraphs mix up the past, the present, and the future. The story takes place in the past. Circle any verbs that are not in past time. Then write the verbs correctly on the lines below.**

I visited a strange garden yesterday. The bushes look like different animals. A giant green elephant watches the main path. I discovered a hidden path. I will follow the trail.

A strange noise sounds behind me. I turned around. The elephant moves! Then the giant plant faces in the other direction.

I decide to leave the weird garden. I try to find my way out. I looked everywhere. The paths twisted and turned.

I turn around again. The elephant watches me. I step farther into the garden. The elephant stared.

Finally, I uncover a hidden gate. I hurry toward it. The elephant appears in front of me. I raced out of the garden. Then I glance back. The garden is gone.

_____  _____  _____  _____

_____  _____  _____  _____

_____  _____  _____  _____

Name _____

# Writing Dialogue

**Write a dialogue, or a conversation between two or more**
**characters in a story.  Try to make the dialogue sound as if**
**real people are talking.  Use quotation marks in your dialogue.**
**Choose one of the following groups**
**of characters for your dialogue:**

► Alan and Miss Hester
► Alan and Abdul Gasazi
► Miss Hester and Abdul Gasazi
► Alan, Miss Hester, and Abdul Gasazi
► Two characters from another story of your choice

_____

_____

_____

_____

_____

_____

_____

_____

_____

_____

_____

_____

Name _____

# Write Quotations Right!

**Rewrite each of the following sentences of dialogue that might have taken place. Add quotation marks, capital letters, or commas.**

1. Miss Hester said please stay with Fritz and give him his afternoon walk.

   _____

   _____

2. don't chew on the furniture, Fritz Alan said angrily.

   _____

   _____

3. please, Fritz Alan exclaimed don't go running off into that garden!

   _____

   _____

4. Alan said if you have Fritz, Mr. Gasazi, would you please give him back?

   _____

   _____

5. something terrible has happened, Miss Hester Alan blurted out. your dog ran away, and Mr. Gasazi turned him into a duck!

   _____

Name _____

# Pig Escape Words!

**Write each word next to its meaning.**

1. to happily roll around in something _____

2. running away in fear _____

3. a big adventure _____

4. a safe place for animals or people _____

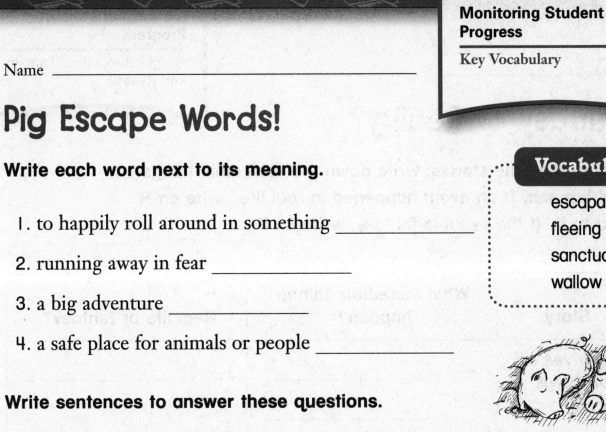

**Write sentences to answer these questions.**

5. Why is a sanctuary an important place for some animals?

_____

6. If you went on an escapade, what do you think you might do?

_____

7. What could happen to make an animal start fleeing?

_____

8. What do pigs like to wallow in?

_____

# Fantasy or Reality?

**As you read the stories, write down the incredible things that happen. If an event happened in real life, write an R next to it. If the event is fantasy, write an F.**

| Story | What incredible things happen? | Real life or fantasy? |
|---|---|---|
| *Fugitives on Four Legs* | 1. _____ <br><br> 2. _____ <br><br> 3. _____ | 1. _____ <br><br> 2. _____ <br><br> 3. _____ |
| *Dinosaur Bob* | 1. _____ <br><br> 2. _____ <br><br> 3. _____ | 1. _____ <br><br> 2. _____ <br><br> 3. _____ |

Name _____

# The Boar Facts

**Think about the selection. Then complete the sentences.**

1. The names of the pigs that escaped were

_____

2. The place where this happened was

_____

3. The amount of time the pigs ran free was

_____ .

4. The pigs' adventures made the news in

_____

5. Today, the pigs live in

_____ .

Name _____

# Travel Words

**Fill each blank with the Key Vocabulary word that best completes the sentence.**

Do you need a vacation? We can find the perfect trip for you!

Would you like to visit Africa? Let us send you on a

_____. You'll see lions, giraffes, and gazelles. Be careful,

though. Lions can be a _____ if you wander alone.

Maybe you'd like a Western vacation instead. You can learn to ride a

horse and sleep under the stars. Around the campfire, you'll be honored

with a singing cowboy _____. Our real-life cowhands

will give you a _____ of "Home on the Range."

How would you like to sail on a big ocean _____?

On the ship you'll stay in a cozy _____, with a bed and

a window. Let us take you wherever you want to go!

Name _____

# Test Practice

**Use the three steps you've learned to write a personal response to these questions about *Dinosaur Bob*. Make a chart on a separate piece of paper, and then write your response on the lines below. Use the checklist to revise your response.**

1. Suppose Dinosaur Bob went on a trip with your family. What might happen? Include many details.

_____

_____

_____

_____

_____

_____

_____

_____

---

**Personal Response Checklist**

✔ Did I restate the question at the beginning?

✔ Can I add more details from what I read to support my answer?

✔ Can I add more of my experiences to support my answer?

✔ Do I need to delete any details that do not help answer the question?

✔ Did I use clear handwriting? Did I make any mistakes?

---

*Continue on page 266.*

Theme 3: **Incredible Stories**     265

## Test Practice continued

2. **Connecting/Comparing** Suppose you could choose either Dinosaur Bob or the dragon in *Raising Dragons* to be your pet. Explain which one you would choose and why.

_____

_____

_____

_____

_____

_____

_____

_____

_____

---

### Personal Response Checklist

✔ Did I restate the question at the beginning?

✔ Can I add more details from what I read to support my answer?

✔ Can I add more of my experiences to support my answer?

✔ Do I need to delete any details that do not help answer the question?

✔ Did I use clear handwriting?  Did I make any mistakes?

---

**Read your answers to Questions I and 2 aloud to a partner. Then discuss the checklist.  Make any changes that will make your answers better.**

Name _____

# Action Plan

**Read the paragraph. Then list the steps on the lines below.**

**Paper Hearts**
**Materials:** construction paper, pencil, scissors
**Directions:** First fold the paper in half. Next draw half of a
heart shape with the straight side on the edge with the fold.
Then cut along the outline. Finally, open the folded paper.

**Steps:**

1. _____

2. _____

3. _____

4. _____

What materials should you gather before beginning the
project?

_____

Why is it important to follow each step in order?

_____

_____

# The Shape of a Story

**Read the story elements listed below from *The Mysterious Giant of Barletta*. Then write the number for each element on the correct line below. More than one number may go on some lines.**

1. An army is coming to destroy the peaceful town of Barletta.
2. Zia Concetta
3. The giant uses an onion to trick the army into leaving the town alone.
4. The peace and quiet disappear as everyone becomes fearful of the army's arrival.
5. the Mysterious Giant
6. a lieutenant
7. Zia asks the giant for assistance and he agrees to help.
8. The giant grabs a large onion and goes to meet the army.
9. Captain Minckion
10. the town of Barletta

Who are the characters in this story? _____

Where does the story take place? _____

What is the story problem? _____

What happens before the problem is solved? _____

What happens to solve the problem? _____

# What's This Word?

**Read the information in the chart. Then unscramble each word below, using what you know about the five prefixes listed in the chart and the clues in parentheses.**

| Prefix | Meaning | Example |
|--------|---------|---------|
| un- | "not" or "the opposite of" | untrue |
| dis- | "not" or "the opposite of" | disappear |
| non- | "not" or "the opposite of" | nonfiction |
| bi- | "two" | bicycle |
| mis- | "wrong" | misbehave |

1. **EIEARGSD**  (fail to agree) _____

2. **DIUETN**  (not tied) _____

3. **SSMUEI**  (use wrongly) _____

4. **YEKLIBEW**  (every two weeks) _____

5. **RDSTUIST**  (opposite of *trust*) _____

6. **PUPDIZEN**  (opposite of *zipped*) _____

7. **OSPONTN**  (without stops) _____

8. **SLIPSLEM**  (spell in a way that is not correct) _____

9. **ENABILP**  (plane with double wings) _____

10. **PYNUAPH**  (not happy) _____

Name _____

# Choose the Correct Meaning

**Read the definitions in the dictionary entries below.**

**bank** (băngk) *noun*  **1.** Ground, often sloping, along the edge of a river, creek, or pond.  **2.** Sideways tilt of an airplane when making a turn.  **3.** Place or container where money is kept.

**ring** (rĭng) *noun*  **1.** The sound made by a bell or other metallic object.  **2.** Any loud sound that is continued or repeated.  **3.** A circle with an empty center.  **4.** A small circular band worn on a finger.

**scan** (skăn) *verb*  **1.** To examine something closely or thoroughly.  **2.** To look something over quickly.

**scout** (skout) *verb*  **1.** To explore a place.  **2.** To observe an athlete for possible hiring by a sports team.

**Read each sentence below.  Choose the correct meaning from the dictionary entries above for each underlined word. Write the number of the correct meaning on the line provided.**

1. We camped inside a ring of pine trees. _____

2. We waded between the steep banks. _____

3. He scouted a way to the top of the hill. _____

4. Looking up for a moment, she scanned the trail ahead.

_____

5. The pilot put the glider into a severe bank to change course.

_____

Name _____

# Spelling Review

**Write each Spelling Word. Then circle six words that are homophone pairs.**

1. _____
2. _____
3. _____
4. _____
5. _____
6. _____
7. _____
8. _____
9. _____
10. _____
11. _____
12. _____

13. _____
14. _____
15. _____
16. _____
17. _____
18. _____
19. _____
20. _____
21. _____
22. _____
23. _____
24. _____
25. _____

## Spelling Words

1. word
2. sound
3. clear
4. also
5. soft
6. crack
7. lawn
8. crown
9. girl
10. knew
11. here
12. turn
13. dark
14. north
15. orange
16. her
17. skin
18. hear
19. squeeze
20. gym
21. second
22. jeans
23. hour
24. our
25. new

Name _____

# Spelling Spree

**Puzzle Play** **Write a Spelling Word for each clue. Then use the letters in the boxes to spell a word about what a dragon is like.**

1. this covers your body ▢ ___ ___ ___

2. first, —, third ___ ___ ▢ ___ ___ ___

3. heavy blue pants ___ ___ ▢ ___ ___

4. 60 minutes ___ ___ ___ ▢

5. a large indoor play area ___ ▢ ___

**Secret Word:** _____

**Picture Clues** **Write Spelling Words for each sentence.**

6–7.  The _____ is holding an _____.

8–9.  Stones from the _____ in the wall are lying on the _____.

10–12. The king, wearing his _____, cannot _____ the soft _____.

**Spelling Words**

1. sound
2. lawn
3. crown
4. girl
5. skin
6. crack
7. gym
8. orange
9. second
10. jeans
11. hear
12. hour

Name _____

# Proofreading and Writing

**Proofreading** Circle the five misspelled Spelling Words below. Write each word correctly.

It can be lonely hear in my big house. I don't hear a werd from morning until darc. This morning, however, I heard a saft sound. It was my friend Masha, who held out a hand for me to skweeze.

| | |
|---|---|
| 1. _____ | 4. _____ |
| 2. _____ | 5. _____ |
| 3. _____ | |

**Which Word?** Write the Spelling Word that best fits each group of words.

6. understood or _____

7. unused or _____

8. in addition _____

9. sunny and _____

10. his or her _____

11. opposite of south _____

12. boy and _____

13. to spin, circle, or _____

14. we, us, _____

**Spelling Words**

1. clear
2. girl
3. turn
4. also
5. squeeze
6. dark
7. soft
8. north
9. her
10. new
11. here
12. our
13. knew
14. word

✏️ **Write Directions** On another sheet of paper, write directions telling the giant how to get from your school to your house. Use the Spelling Review Words.

Name _____

# Writing Possessives

**On the line provided, write the correct possessive form of the noun in parentheses to complete each sentence. Then write *S* if the possessive noun is singular and *P* if it is plural.**

1. The _____ escapade began on market day in

   Malmesbury, England. (pigs) _____

2. They spoiled a _____ plan by escaping from

   him. (butcher) _____

3. The two pigs trotted through _____ fields.

   (farmers) _____

4. They rooted around in _____ gardens.

   (families) _____

5. These plump animals avoided a _____ net.

   (policeman) _____

6. They became the _____ favorite pigs.

   (country) _____

Name _____

# Writing Past and Future

**Read each sentence. Then write the sentence in past time and future time.**

1. Scotty returns with a dinosaur.

   Past: _____

   Future: _____

2. Bob carries the family down the river.

   Past: _____

   Future: _____

3. Zelda plays baseball with the others.

   Past: _____

   Future: _____

4. The family sails on a big ship.

   Past: _____

   Future: _____

5. Passengers dance on Bob's back.

   Past: _____

   Future: _____

# Student Handbook

# Contents

**Spelling**

**Grammar and Usage**

# How to Study a Word

## 1. LOOK at the word.
► What does the word mean?
► What letters are in the word?
► Name and touch each letter.

## 2. SAY the word.
► Listen for the consonant sounds.
► Listen for the vowel sounds.

## 3. THINK about the word.
► How is each sound spelled?
► Close your eyes and picture the word.
► What familiar spelling patterns do you see?
► What other words have the same spelling patterns?

## 4. WRITE the word.
► Think about the sounds and the letters.
► Form the letters correctly.

## 5. CHECK the spelling.
► Did you spell the word the same way it is spelled in your word list?
► If you did not spell the word correctly, write the word again.

| | | | | |
|---|---|---|---|---|
| about | don't | I'd | | |
| again | down | I'll | | |
| almost | | I'm | outside | tonight |
| a lot | enough | into | | too |
| also | every | its | people | two |
| always | everybody | it's | pretty | |
| am | | | | until |
| and | family | January | really | |
| another | favorite | | right | very |
| anyone | February | knew | | |
| anyway | field | know | said | want |
| around | finally | | Saturday | was |
| | for | letter | school | Wednesday |
| beautiful | found | like | some | we're |
| because | friend | little | something | where |
| been | from | lose | started | while |
| before | | lying | stopped | who |
| brought | getting | | sure | whole |
| buy | girl | might | swimming | world |
| | goes | morning | | would |
| cannot | going | mother | than | wouldn't |
| can't | guess | myself | that's | write |
| clothes | | | their | writing |
| coming | happily | never | them | |
| could | have | new | then | you |
| cousin | haven't | now | there | your |
| | heard | | they | |
| does | her | off | thought | |
| didn't | here | one | through | |
| different | his | other | to | |
| done | how | our | today | |

## The Ballad of Mulan

### More Short Vowels
/ŏ/ ➔ lot
/ŭ/ ➔ rub

### Spelling Words
1. pond
2. luck
3. drop
4. lot
5. rub
6. does
7. drum
8. sock
9. hunt
10. crop
11. shut
12. won

### Challenge Words
1. dodge
2. dusk

**My Study List**
Add your own spelling words on the back. ➔

## Off to Adventure!
### Reading-Writing Workshop

**Look for familiar spelling patterns in these words to help you remember their spellings.**

### Spelling Words
1. have
2. haven't
3. found
4. around
5. one
6. than
7. then
8. them
9. before
10. because
11. other
12. mother

### Challenge Words
1. family
2. cousin
3. everybody
4. guess

**My Study List**
Add your own spelling words on the back. ➔

## Cliff Hanger

### Short Vowels
/ă/ ➔ last
/ĕ/ ➔ smell
/ĭ/ ➔ mix

### Spelling Words
1. mix
2. milk
3. smell
4. last
5. head
6. friend
7. class
8. left
9. thick
10. send
11. thin
12. stick

### Challenge Words
1. empty
2. glance

**My Study List**
Add your own spelling words on the back. ➔

## Take-Home Word List

## Take-Home Word List

Name _____

### My Study List

1. _____
2. _____
3. _____
4. _____
5. _____
6. _____
7. _____
8. _____
9. _____
10. _____

### Review Words

1. test
2. dish

### How to Study a Word

**Look** at the word.
**Say** the word.
**Think** about the word.
**Write** the word.
**Check** the spelling.

Name _____

### My Study List

1. _____
2. _____
3. _____
4. _____
5. _____
6. _____
7. _____
8. _____
9. _____
10. _____

### How to Study a Word

**Look** at the word.
**Say** the word.
**Think** about the word.
**Write** the word.
**Check** the spelling.

Name _____

### My Study List

1. _____
2. _____
3. _____
4. _____
5. _____
6. _____
7. _____
8. _____
9. _____
10. _____

### Review Words

1. hop
2. much

### How to Study a Word

**Look** at the word.
**Say** the word.
**Think** about the word.
**Write** the word.
**Check** the spelling.

## The Keeping Quilt

**More Long Vowel Spellings**

/ā/ ➡ p**ai**nt, cl**ay**

/ē/ ➡ l**ea**ve, f**ee**l

### Spelling Words

1. paint
2. clay
3. feel
4. leave
5. neighbor
6. eight
7. seem
8. speak
9. paid
10. lay
11. need
12. weigh

### Challenge Words

1. needle
2. crayon

**My Study List**
Add your own spelling words on the back. ➡

## Off to Adventure!
### Spelling Review

### Spelling Words

1. last
2. mix
3. stick
4. lot
5. sock
6. hunt
7. wide
8. grade
9. thick
10. send
11. class
12. pond
13. luck
14. drum
15. save
16. cube
17. smile
18. left
19. smell
20. thin
21. drop
22. shut
23. huge
24. note
25. life

### See the back for Challenge Words.

**My Study List**
Add your own spelling words on the back. ➡

## The Lost and Found

**The Vowel-Consonant-*e* Pattern**

/ā/ ➡ s**a**v**e**

/ī/ ➡ l**i**f**e**

/ō/ ➡ sm**o**k**e**

/yōo/ ➡ h**u**g**e**

### Spelling Words

1. smoke
2. huge
3. save
4. life
5. wide
6. come
7. mine
8. grade
9. smile
10. note
11. cube
12. love

### Challenge Words

1. escape
2. slope

**My Study List**
Add your own spelling words on the back. ➡

## Take-Home Word List

## Take-Home Word List

## Take-Home Word List

Name _____

Name _____

Name _____

### My Study List

1. _____
2. _____
3. _____
4. _____
5. _____
6. _____
7. _____
8. _____
9. _____
10. _____

### My Study List

1. _____
2. _____
3. _____
4. _____
5. _____
6. _____
7. _____
8. _____
9. _____
10. _____

### My Study List

1. _____
2. _____
3. _____
4. _____
5. _____
6. _____
7. _____
8. _____
9. _____
10. _____

### Review Words

1. test
2. dish

### Challenge Words

1. glance
2. empty
3. dusk
4. slope
5. escape

### Review Words

1. clean
2. play

### How to Study a Word

**Look** at the word.
**Say** the word.
**Think** about the word.
**Write** the word.
**Check** the spelling.

### How to Study a Word

**Look** at the word.
**Say** the word.
**Think** about the word.
**Write** the word.
**Check** the spelling.

### How to Study a Word

**Look** at the word.
**Say** the word.
**Think** about the word.
**Write** the word.
**Check** the spelling.

## The Talking Cloth

**Three-Letter Clusters and Unexpected Consonant Patterns**
**spr**ing
**str**eet
**thr**ow
/n/ ➝ **kn**ee
/r/ ➝ **wr**ap
/ch/ ➝ wa**tch**

### Spelling Words

1. spring
2. knee
3. throw
4. patch
5. strong
6. wrap
7. three
8. watch
9. street
10. know
11. spread
12. write

### Challenge Words

1. strength
2. kitchen

**My Study List**
Add your own spelling words on the back. ➝

285

## Grandma's Records

**The Long *o* Sound**
/ō/ ➝ c**oa**ch, bl**ow**, h**o**ld

### Spelling Words

1. coach
2. blow
3. float
4. hold
5. sew
6. though
7. sold
8. soap
9. row
10. own
11. both
12. most

### Challenge Words

1. tomorrow
2. program

**My Study List**
Add your own spelling words on the back. ➝

285

## Celebrating Traditions
### Reading-Writing Workshop

**Look for familiar spelling patterns in these words to help you remember their spellings.**

### Spelling Words

1. now
2. off
3. for
4. almost
5. also
6. can't
7. cannot
8. about
9. always
10. today
11. until
12. again

### Challenge Words

1. February
2. January
3. Saturday
4. Wednesday

**My Study List**
Add your own spelling words on the back. ➝

285

## Take-Home Word List

Name _____

### ✏️ My Study List

1. _____
2. _____
3. _____
4. _____
5. _____
6. _____
7. _____
8. _____
9. _____
10. _____

### How to Study a Word

**Look** at the word.
**Say** the word.
**Think** about the word.
**Write** the word.
**Check** the spelling.

286

## Take-Home Word List

Name _____

### ✏️ My Study List

1. _____
2. _____
3. _____
4. _____
5. _____
6. _____
7. _____
8. _____
9. _____
10. _____

### Review Words

1. cold
2. slow

### How to Study a Word

**Look** at the word.
**Say** the word.
**Think** about the word.
**Write** the word.
**Check** the spelling.

286

## Take-Home Word List

Name _____

### ✏️ My Study List

1. _____
2. _____
3. _____
4. _____
5. _____
6. _____
7. _____
8. _____
9. _____
10. _____

### Review Words

1. catch
2. two

### How to Study a Word

**Look** at the word.
**Say** the word.
**Think** about the word.
**Write** the word.
**Check** the spelling.

286

### Dogzilla

**The Vowel Sounds in *clown* and *lawn***

/ou/ ➛ cl**ow**n, s**ou**nd

/ô/ ➛ l**aw**n, cl**o**th, t**a**lk

### Spelling Words

1. clown
2. lawn
3. talk
4. sound
5. cloth
6. would
7. also
8. mouth
9. crown
10. soft
11. count
12. law

### Challenge Words

1. bounce
2. officer

**My Study List**
Add your own spelling words on the back. ➛

### Celebrating Traditions
### Spelling Review

### Spelling Words

1. speak
2. feel
3. seem
4. most
5. both
6. know
7. street
8. lie
9. need
10. paint
11. hold
12. float
13. three
14. spread
15. mind
16. might
17. lay
18. leave
19. own
20. row
21. wrap
22. patch
23. tie
24. wild
25. bright

### See the back for Challenge Words.

**My Study List**
Add your own spelling words on the back. ➛

### Dancing Rainbows

**The Long *i* Sound**

/ī/ ➛ br**igh**t, w**i**ld, d**ie**

### Spelling Words

1. wild
2. bright
3. die
4. sight
5. child
6. pie
7. fight
8. lie
9. tight
10. tie
11. might
12. mind

### Challenge Words

1. design
2. delight

**My Study List**
Add your own spelling words on the back. ➛

## Take-Home Word List

## Take-Home Word List

## Take-Home Word List

Name _____

Name _____

Name _____

### My Study List

1. _____
2. _____
3. _____
4. _____
5. _____
6. _____
7. _____
8. _____
9. _____
10. _____

### My Study List

1. _____
2. _____
3. _____
4. _____
5. _____
6. _____
7. _____
8. _____
9. _____
10. _____

### My Study List

1. _____
2. _____
3. _____
4. _____
5. _____
6. _____
7. _____
8. _____
9. _____
10. _____

### Review Words

1. find
2. high

### Challenge Words

1. needle
2. tomorrow
3. program
4. kitchen
5. design

### Review Words

1. town
2. small

### How to Study a Word

**Look** at the word.
**Say** the word.
**Think** about the word.
**Write** the word.
**Check** the spelling.

### How to Study a Word

**Look** at the word.
**Say** the word.
**Think** about the word.
**Write** the word.
**Check** the spelling.

### How to Study a Word

**Look** at the word.
**Say** the word.
**Think** about the word.
**Write** the word.
**Check** the spelling.

## Raising Dragons

**The /j/, /k/, and /kw/ Sounds**

/j/ → jeans, large, gym

/k/ → park, quick, picnic

/kw/ → quick

### Spelling Words

1. large
2. gym
3. skin
4. quick
5. picnic
6. judge
7. park
8. jeans
9. crack
10. orange
11. second
12. squeeze

### Challenge Words

1. courage
2. insect

**My Study List**
Add your own spelling words on the back. →

## The Mysterious Giant of Barletta

**Vowel + /r/ Sounds**

/är/ → dark

/î\r/ → clear

/ôr/ → north

/ûr/ → her, girl, turn, work

### Spelling Words

1. girl
2. clear
3. her
4. turn
5. dark
6. work
7. smart
8. word
9. hurt
10. serve
11. north
12. third

### Challenge Words

1. tornado
2. scurried

**My Study List**
Add your own spelling words on the back. →

## Incredible Stories
## Reading-Writing Workshop

Look for familiar spelling patterns in these words to help you remember their spellings.

### Spelling Words

1. and
2. said
3. goes
4. going
5. some
6. something
7. you
8. your
9. friend
10. school
11. where
12. myself

### Challenge Words

1. tonight
2. lying
3. field
4. enough

**My Study List**
Add your own spelling words on the back. →

## Take-Home Word List

### My Study List

1. _____
2. _____
3. _____
4. _____
5. _____
6. _____
7. _____
8. _____
9. _____
10. _____

## Take-Home Word List

### My Study List

1. _____
2. _____
3. _____
4. _____
5. _____
6. _____
7. _____
8. _____
9. _____
10. _____

### Review Words

1. hard
2. morning

## Take-Home Word List

### My Study List

1. _____
2. _____
3. _____
4. _____
5. _____
6. _____
7. _____
8. _____
9. _____
10. _____

### Review Words

1. rock
2. job

### How to Study a Word

**Look** at the word.
**Say** the word.
**Think** about the word.
**Write** the word.
**Check** the spelling.

### How to Study a Word

**Look** at the word.
**Say** the word.
**Think** about the word.
**Write** the word.
**Check** the spelling.

### How to Study a Word

**Look** at the word.
**Say** the word.
**Think** about the word.
**Write** the word.
**Check** the spelling.

## Incredible Stories
## Spelling Review

### Spelling Words

1. sound
2. crown
3. word
4. her
5. crack
6. orange
7. hear
8. our
9. also
10. girl
11. dark
12. clear
13. squeeze
14. second
15. here
16. new
17. soft
18. turn
19. north
20. skin
21. gym
22. jeans
23. hour
24. knew
25. lawn

**See the back for Challenge Words**

**My Study List**
Add your own spelling words on the back. ➡

## The Garden of Abdul Gasazi

**Homophones**
Homophones are words that sound alike but have different spellings and meanings.

### Spelling Words

1. hear
2. here
3. new
4. knew
5. its
6. it's
7. our
8. hour
9. there
10. their
11. they're

### Challenge Words

1. seen
2. scene

**My Study List**
Add your own spelling words on the back. ➡

Take-Home Word List

## Take-Home Word List

Name _____

### My Study List

1. _____
2. _____
3. _____
4. _____
5. _____
6. _____
7. _____
8. _____
9. _____
10. _____

### Review Words

1. eye
2. I

### How to Study a Word

**Look** at the word.
**Say** the word.
**Think** about the word.
**Write** the word.
**Check** the spelling.

Name _____

### My Study List

1. _____
2. _____
3. _____
4. _____
5. _____
6. _____
7. _____
8. _____
9. _____
10. _____

### Challenge Words

1. officer
2. scurried
3. insect
4. seen
5. scene

### How to Study a Word

**Look** at the word.
**Say** the word.
**Think** about the word.
**Write** the word.
**Check** the spelling.

## Focus on Trickster Tales

| The Vowel Sound in *join* |
|---|
| /oi/ ➡ j**oi**n, j**oy** |

### Spelling Words

1. join
2. joy
3. boil
4. noise
5. spoil
6. choice
7. soil
8. point
9. foil
10. voice
11. coil
12. broil

### Challenge Words

1. enjoy
2. rejoice

**My Study List**
Add your own spelling words on the back. ➡

## Focus on Poetry

| More Short and Long Vowels |
|---|
| short vowel sounds ➡ st**a**nd, r**e**st, tw**i**st, cl**o**ck, st**u**ff |
| long vowel sounds ➡ pl**ate**, wh**ite**, sp**oke**, J**une** |

### Spelling Words

1. stand
2. rest
3. plate
4. clock
5. white
6. stuff
7. spoke
8. bend
9. frame
10. twist
11. June
12. mile

### Challenge Words

1. liquid
2. decide

**My Study List**
Add your own spelling words on the back. ➡

Name _____

## My Study List

1. _____
2. _____
3. _____
4. _____
5. _____
6. _____
7. _____
8. _____
9. _____
10. _____

### Review Words

1. when
2. back

### How to Study a Word

**Look** at the word.
**Say** the word.
**Think** about the word.
**Write** the word.
**Check** the spelling.

Name _____

## My Study List

1. _____
2. _____
3. _____
4. _____
5. _____
6. _____
7. _____
8. _____
9. _____
10. _____

### Review Words

1. coin
2. boy

### How to Study a Word

**Look** at the word.
**Say** the word.
**Think** about the word.
**Write** the word.
**Check** the spelling.

# Problem Words

| Words | Rules | Examples |
|---|---|---|
| are<br>our | *Are* is a verb.<br>*Our* is a possessive pronoun. | <u>Are</u> these gloves yours?<br>This is <u>our</u> car. |
| doesn't<br><br>don't | Use *doesn't* with singular nouns, *he*, *she*, and *it*.<br>Use *don't* with plural nouns, *I*, *you*, *we*, and *they*. | Dad <u>doesn't</u> swim.<br><br>We <u>don't</u> swim. |
| good<br><br>well | Use the adjective *good* to describe nouns.<br>Use the adverb *well* to describe verbs. | The weather looks <u>good</u>.<br><br>She sings <u>well</u>. |
| its<br>it's | *Its* is a possessive pronoun.<br>*It's* means "it is" (contraction). | The dog wagged <u>its</u> tail.<br><u>It's</u> cold today. |
| let<br>leave | *Let* means "to allow."<br>*Leave* means "to go away from" or "to let stay." | Please <u>let</u> me go swimming.<br>I will <u>leave</u> soon.<br><u>Leave</u> it on my desk. |
| set<br>sit | *Set* means "to put."<br>*Sit* means "to rest or stay in one place." | <u>Set</u> the vase on the table.<br>Please <u>sit</u> in this chair. |
| their<br>there<br>they're | *Their* means "belonging to them."<br>*There* means "at or in that place."<br>*They're* means "they are" (contraction). | <u>Their</u> coats are on the bed.<br>Is Carlos <u>there</u>?<br><u>They're</u> going to the store. |
| two<br>to<br><br>too | *Two* is a number<br>*To* means "toward."<br>*Too* means "also" or "more than enough." | I bought <u>two</u> shirts.<br>A cat ran <u>to</u> the tree.<br>Can we go <u>too</u>?<br>I ate <u>too</u> many peas. |
| your<br>you're | *Your* is a possessive pronoun.<br>*You're* means "you are" (contraction). | Are these <u>your</u> glasses?<br><u>You're</u> late again! |

Read each question below.  Then check your paper.  Correct any mistakes you find.  After you have corrected them, put a check mark in the box next to the question.

☐    1. Did I indent each paragraph?

☐    2. Does each sentence tell one complete thought?

☐    3. Did I end each sentence with the correct end mark?

☐    4. Did I begin each sentence with a capital letter?

☐    5. Did I use capital letters correctly in other places?

☐    6. Did I use commas correctly?

☐    7. Did I spell all the words the right way?

Are there other problem areas you should watch for?  Make your own proofreading checklist.

☐ _____

☐ _____

☐ _____

☐ _____

☐ _____

☐ _____

☐ _____

# Proofreading Marks

| Mark | Explanation | Examples |
|------|-------------|----------|
| ¶ | Begin a new paragraph. Indent the paragraph. | ¶The boat finally arrived. It was two hours late. |
| ∧ | Add letters, words, or sentences. | My ^best^ friend ate lunch with me t^o^day. |
| ℘ | Take out words, sentences, and punctuation marks. Correct spelling. | We ~~looked at and~~ admired, the modd^e^l airplanes. |
| ≡ | Change a small letter to a capital letter. | New York c̲i̲t̲y is exciting. |
| / | Change a capital letter to a small letter. | The /Fireflies blinked in the dark. |
| ⟨⟨ ⟩⟩ | Add quotation marks. | ⟨⟨Where do you want the piano?⟩⟩ asked the movers. |
| ∧ | Add a comma. | Carlton˄my cat˄has a mind of his own. |
| ⊙ | Add a period. | Put a period at the end of the sentence⊙ |
| ∼ | Reverse letters or words. | Ra∼ed carefully the instructions! |
| ? | Add a question mark. | Should I put the mark here? |
| ! | Add an exclamation mark. | Look out below! |

_____

_____

_____

_____

_____

_____

_____

_____

_____

_____

_____

_____

_____

_____

_____

_____